STARTING
CYCLE ROAD RACING AND TIME TRIALS

STARTING CYCLE ROAD RACING AND TIME TRIALS

Mark Barfield

Dr Auriel Forrester

THE CROWOOD PRESS

First published in 2008 by
The Crowood Press Ltd
Ramsbury, Marlborough
Wiltshire SN8 2HR

www.crowood.com

British Library Cataloguing-in-Publication Data
A catalogue record for this book is available from the British Library.

ISBN 978 1 84797 014 5

All photographs are by and copyright of Jonathan Forrester, except where otherwise credited.

Disclaimer
Please note that the authors and the publisher of this book are not responsible in any manner whatsoever for any damage, or injury of any kind, that may result from practising or applying, the techniques and methods and/or following the instructions described in this publication. Since the physical activites described in this book may be too strenuous in nature for some readers to engage in safely. It is essential that a dotor be consulted prior to undertaking training and cycling activities of any kind.

Designed and typeset by
Focus Publishing Ltd,
Sevenoaks, Kent

Printed and bound in
Singapore by Craft Print
International Ltd

CONTENTS

CHAPTER 1
Introduction

THE HISTORY OF
THE BICYCLE

The bicycle has been around in a recognisable form since the eighteenth century, but the timeline of the history of bicycles remains uncertain. Sources often disagree as to the names of the inventors and the dates of their inventions. Leonardo da Vinci supposedly sketched what could be recognized as a modern bicycle in 1490 and around 1790 a Frenchman, the Comte de Sivrac, developed a *célérifère*, which had two in-line wheels connected by a beam. The rider straddled the beam and propelled the *célérifère* by pushing his feet on the ground, in scooter fashion. This machine became known as the 'hobby horse'. In 1817, German Baron Karl von Drais added steering. Several versions appeared around France and England in the early 1800s. As a replacement for the horse, these 'hobby horses' were a short-lived craze. The roads of the time hindered the development of wheeled transport of this type.

Scottish blacksmith Kirkpatrick MacMillan developed a rear-drive bike in 1839 using a treadle and rod for the rear-drive mechanism. He rode more than 60 miles (95km) to Glasgow on it, but the machine's popularity didn't spread beyond the Scottish borders. R.W. Thompson patented a pneumatic tube in 1845. Prior to this invention, bikes had metal wheels, which made for uncomfortable riding over what were undoubtedly not smooth roads.

The French argue that the father and son team of Pierre and Ernest Michaux were the inventors of the modern bicycle, when in the 1860s they presented their *vélocipède*, which boasted a metal frame, cranks and pedals. It had a larger front wheel which made it faster, but less stable. A bicycle boom ensued for a while in France.

British engineers were next to pick up the design and improve upon it by adding ball bearings, pneumatic (Dunlop) tyres, wire-spoked wheels, chain drive, variable gears and cable controls.

Over a twenty-year span, the British brought the bicycle to its present form, thanks mainly to John Starley of the Coventry Sewing Machine Company. In 1885, after forming the Starley and Sutton Company with local cycling enthusiast William Sutton, the Starley Rover Safety Bicycle was born, returning wheels to a reasonable size after the perilous Penny Farthing, with its large front wheel and much smaller rear one, and improving the bike's stability. In the early days, newspapers railed against the two-wheel speedsters, but with the invention of the safety bicycle and manufacturing processes which made the bicycle more affordable, the popularity of the bicycle has spread exponentially, until the present the day when it has come to play a huge part in many people's lives around the globe.

CYCLING AS A SPORT

As is often the case, the competitive aspect of human nature quickly came to the fore and cycle sports were born. The history of cycle sport in the UK, as well as around the world, is worthy of a book in its own right. Cycling's popularity has fluctuated over the years, having been stimulated by events of colossal distances and challenges of endurance which make modern sport look

A road racer in action – the effort is clear.

easy in comparison. Well-documented events spanning hundreds of kilometres in one go and races lasting six days still cast an influence over modern cycle sport, although we now exist in a world that is slightly less obsessed with the impossible.

Modern cycle sports are divided up into a number of different areas for competition purposes:

- Track racing is, as the name suggests, racing that takes place on a closed, usually steeply banked track, or velodrome. Races differ in length, from true sprint events up to longer endurance and group racing events. This form of cycle sport is exciting to watch and easy to identify with, although the action can sometimes be tricky to follow in the more complex events.
- Off-road racing is an umbrella term for a wide number of events. Traditionally, it consisted of Cyclo-Cross, a winter sport using bikes that to the untrained eye looked like road bikes but had some subtle but important adaptations to accommo-date the conditions. Over the past two decades, Cyclo-Cross has been joined by mountain biking. There are a number of forms of mountain bike racing, from the self-explanatory cross-country racing, which takes place with large groups racing in a first-across-the-line event, to downhill mountain biking, which is, as the name suggests, a race from the top of a hill or climb to the bottom. This can be run as a time trial or a head-to-head competition, which is very exciting to watch but deceiv-ingly difficult to do. Off-road racing also includes BMX racing. BMX has recently been accepted as an Olympic discipline and as such the profile of BMX racing has increased, with many countries now dedi-

Time trial – the solo effort.

cating time and resources to encouraging this sport, which started as a pastime in the late 1980s. BMX competition can also encompass the freestyle element, including fascinating stunts and tricks. These are widely practised, although formal competition is less easy to find.

- Road racing is the term that is often used to describe mass-start group races on roads. The road may be part of the highway, or a motor-racing circuit, or a purpose-built cycling circuit.
- Time trials are commonly used as a component stage of a longer stage race and you will often hear of races starting with a prologue time trial, which is a shorter time trial to get the race started. There are national championships in all cycling nations including time trials, but in the UK time trialling has a profile within the sport that it does not enjoy across Europe.

For the uninitiated, the Tour de France is often the only reference point for cycle sport on the road. Le Tour is a stage race taking place over three weeks and is the most recognizable of cycling events. It is attractive in as much as the best equipment is on show and the best road riders in the world, supported by the best teams, are presented to the public during the race, as it is the most important event for any sponsor involved in cycle sport. Today's media ensures that regardless or where you are in the world you are likely to be able to see Le Tour on television or follow its progress via the Internet.

There are two other races of similar magnitude, one in Spain and one in Italy. Stage racing is great for the media as it provides daily dramas and a long-playing story, with fans being updated on a daily basis. The opportunities for novices to take part in stage races are limited, however, although there are several entry level races of this type in the UK and Europe which can provide a glimpse of the effort required, albeit normally over three days rather than three weeks.

At the professional and elite level, cycle sport on the road includes many smaller stage

The amateur peloton (main pack) passing through.

races and one-day races. The portfolio of events across Europe is extensive and includes many events that have histories to rival the Tour de France, including the Tour of Flanders (Ronde van Vlaanderen) and the Paris-Roubaix. These events attract very loyal local followings and are often won by riders who wouldn't necessarily shine in the overall standings of the national tours.

The beating heart of cycle sport is in Europe, with Belgium, France, Italy, Spain and Holland leading the way. Recently, this group has been augmented by a large swathe of riders from the old East Germany and from ex-Eastern bloc countries. Australians and Americans have also made a significant impact on the European cycling scene. In addition, there are events around the world that the top teams and associated media interest outside of the established road cycling season. However, despite these changes and the influence that the legendary

seven-times winner of the Tour de France, the American Lance Armstrong, has had on cycling, the sport remains strongest in Central Europe. The history of British riders in Europe is chequered, but there is a steady stream of Brits heading across the Channel to chance their arm as full-time riders. Belgium and France remain the easiest targets and there are many opportunities to race, thus ensuring that the ambitious rider can obtain as much experience as possible.

Cycle sport in Britain is healthy and diverse, with most towns and cities having good cycling clubs in addition to a rich collection of races being promoted across the country throughout the racing season, which stretches from March through to mid-October. The focus of this book is cycle racing on the road and by reading it you will be taking one of the first steps to entering this exciting, healthy and exhilarating pastime. Whilst the Tour de France represents the pinnacle of a profes-

A standard road race bike.

Chasing the break.

sional cyclist's career, there are many other, more accessible, forms of competitive road cycling that will allow any reasonably fit individual with a bit of determination and a little effort to experience the unique sporting experience that is cycle sport on the road.

The aim of this book is to open the door to the novice. Cycling can often be seen as a secret world with its own language and code and a confusing array of references that everybody seems to know but you. This book will guide you through everything you will need to know and do in order to get involved in racing bicycles on the road. We will cover the equipment you will need to get started and help you to get your bike set up so that you can be as competitive as possible. This is often a very daunting aspect of cycling, as equipment can be a substantial investment. With a little guidance, we hope to show you how to get value for money and obtain equipment that will be fit for purpose as well as exciting and enjoyable to use. There is a vast array of equipment available to the enthusiast and, as with many areas of life, competitive cycling equipment is subject to the laws of fashion. We will therefore present

the equipment that is essential, the equipment that is nice to have and the equipment that is probably more of an indulgence than anything else. You can put a very good rider on a very poorly set-up bike and that rider will perform poorly, or you can put an average rider on a bike set up to optimize their performance and they will perform well and enjoy it. When a bike is set up well, the power is transferred as efficiently as possible from the muscles to the mechanical components of the bike. This energy is then transmitted to the road to produce forward motion. A poor set-up will waste energy and be uncomfortable. Examples of competitive cyclists who do not follow the basic guidelines that are tried and tested and published in this book for your advantage can be seen at any gathering of cyclists. Poor position is just one of the things that can make cycling less of a pleasure. A correct and suitable position will give you the best mix of efficiency and comfort, ensuring that every tiny bit of fitness and conditioning that you will undoubtedly have worked very hard to obtain is capitalized upon and not wasted just for the sake of a minor adjustment in position.

You will also discover within these pages the skills required to take part in cycle sport on the road, a surprise to some who may think it's just about pedalling harder and faster! There are many techniques that will ensure you can ride safely, efficiently and effectively, both in training and in racing, whether this is in a mass-participation 'group' race, which from this point we will describe as a road race, or in an individual or team time trial. These techniques will cover the basics involved in riding a bicycle safely, moving through to advanced bike handling and racing techniques. Again, as with position, technique can make the difference between enjoyable riding and tedious slogging. Understanding the techniques of racing will help you to become as efficient and effective as possible during a race, ensuring that your efforts are not wasted and energy is not expended needlessly. We will advise you on how to practise these techniques and how to work technique sessions into your overall training.

We will also look at how to train for your chosen type of racing. There are many myths regarding training for cycling events. Conversations with experienced cyclists will reveal a myriad of training techniques and stories that may only contribute to confusion. We will explain the training process, as well as how to plan it and fit it into a busy lifestyle. A systematic approach to training is vital in order to make the most of your available time. You will learn how to design and structure your training sessions around a goal, event or a performance standard and how to monitor your personal improvements and efforts.

Once you are heading towards the right physical condition to race, this book will explain how to plan participation in your chosen event, from working out where to find details of races, through to how to enter an event and what to expect as the big day gets a bit nearer. We will also look at the rules you need to observe to ensure you can compete fairly and don't incur the wrath of the race officials and commissaires. We will detail the race tactics and strategies that can help the novice to have a good race and give the aspiring rider the best possible chance of achieving a good performance.

Time Trialling

There are two main types of cycle racing on the road – time trialling and road racing. Time trialling is the simplest and arguably the most accessible form of cycle sport on the road. It involves riders being set off on a pre-established course, often over standard distances of 10, 25, 50 or 100 miles (16, 40, 80 or 160km) with the sole objective of completing the course as quickly as possible. There are also many events consisting of a non-standard distance, with an increase in the number of events that are described as 'sporting'. This usually means a circuit-based event, which involves a test of bike handling skills, not just fitness and form. There are also hilly or mountainous events that enable those naturally gifted climbers to excel and prove their abilities over more undulating courses.

There are hundreds of events across the UK throughout the year, nowadays extending beyond the traditional cycling season of March to September. There are even events on Boxing Day and New Year's Day for those preferring a less traditional festive period. Many local clubs run events on weekday evenings and whilst it can be tricky to find published details, a quick word with a member of a local club or the owner of a racing-oriented cycle shop should point you in the right direction. These events are small, low key events run by clubs on courses close to their meeting place. In the main riders will all be from the same club plus maybe a few newcomers like yourself or from other nearby clubs. The club events will be over the same course on a weekly basis throughout the season and there will often be no more organization than a car parked up and used for signing on plus a couple of timekeepers. The entry fee for these events ranges from as little as fifty pence to rarely more than a few pounds, which is excellent value for money for a competitive cycling event. The only requirement is that you are a member of a cycling club that is affiliated to the national governing body for time trials in the UK,

Cornering at speed.

Cycling Time Trials (CTT), which was previously known as the Road Time Trials Council (RTTC).

The other type of time trials is open events. These events are, as the name suggests, open to all participants, though there is still a requirement to be a member of a club affiliated to the CTT. Compared with club events, these are higher profile events with riders from all over the country entering in advance. The entry fees are higher, the courses are often on more major roads and there is often price money at stake – much better to make this your goal event and start off by practising and training at the more social club events. The CTT publishes

a handbook every year, which is available from its head office (see Appendix).This handbook details the location of the events and the race organizer. To enter, you will need to complete the necessary form; you then receive your starting information and are ready to race. These open events will probably be the best ones to plan into your calendar as they are at fixed points during the year. The handbook is available from early each new year and so can be a valuable planning tool to help you to schedule your training plan up to and including your chosen event.

There are also team time trials in different formats. This discipline is a superb way to enjoy racing in a safe and low-cost way. Team time trials are run over varying distances, although they are generally slightly longer than the 10-mile (16km) time trial, .effort simply because you are spurred on by the riders around you. The times you will achieve working as a well-organized team will be much better than your solo times and the sense of achievement will be shared amongst all team members, making this form of time trialling a completely different experience to racing on your own.

Road Racing

Whilst time trialling is the biggest form of cycle sport in the UK, with many riders specializing in time trials exclusively, it is road racing that is recognized by the public as the more high-profile form of cycle sport, due to its association with the Tour de France. The excitement of racing shoulder to shoulder with others should be experienced by any cycling fan, although road racing is arguably a more difficult form of cycle sport to become involved in as you must be able to keep up with the bunch to stay in the race. Despite the ranking and category system in place in the UK, it is still necessary to possess a good level of fitness and skill in order to stay with a race. However, with good training, practice and dedication it is possible to get into road racing and become competitive within a relatively short space of time. It is not always the strongest rider who wins a road race and it is this combination of strength, tactics and skills that make road racing exciting, challenging and rewarding.

Road racing in the UK is governed by British Cycling (see Appendix), although unlike time trialling if you just want to try one race you can often turn up and pay an additional day fee (for both a licence and membership) and race, although if you plan to race more than a handful of times in any given year membership of British Cycling is highly recommended, especially as it will also include third-party liability insurance. British Cycling publishes a yearly handbook, as well as listing its registered events on its comprehensive website, which means that you can find a race near you months in advance and plan your training accordingly. Road racing in the UK is organized into categories based upon ability, with the lowest category being fourth, up through third and second, to first category and finally elite. It is suggested that you aim for fourth or third initially. The race information on the website or in the handbook will detail the start time, race distances and race organizer.

It is always worth giving the organizer a call to ask about the nature of the course. There are not many events that are run on the open road with full road closure, so it is necessary to keep your wits about you when competing. However, there are also an increasing number of closed road circuits specifically designed for cycle racing, or motor racing circuits may be used for road racing. These provide a closed-road feel and a safe environment, which can lead to a very competitive event. Closed-circuit race events are ideal for the novice, as they allow plenty of space for minor mistakes to be made. Also, should you be unfortunate enough to get dropped off the back of the group, because of a mechanical failure, a puncture, or because you are struggling with the pace, you can rejoin when the group comes back round. The race officials will generally allow this, as they want to encourage new people to race and compete.

There are also races that take place over a number of stages. In the UK, for categories lower than first and elite these are generally restarted to a weekend with three or four stages. This kind of race can be something to aim for, as it will test your ability, skills, stamina and strength to the limit. It will also provide you with an experience that you can really compare to the grand European tours such as the Tours of France, Italy and Spain. Road races are generally organized at weekends, although during the summer months races are often listed in the evenings. Combined with the programme offered by time trialling, it is possible to compete almost every day of the week.

Whilst the majority of road races in the UK are organized under the guidance and subsequent insurance provided by British

A local time trial – open to all.

Cycling registration, other organizations are also active. It is possible to take part in age-related races, for example those run by the League International. These races are normally organized under a handicap system, with the younger rider starting last and the older riders getting the advantage of setting off first and being chased. Such races provide a good starting point for the older novice. There is also an organization called the League of Veteran Racing Cyclists, which runs races for riders over forty years old, with prizes and recognition for performances in age groups from forty upwards in five-year age categories. The racing is well structured and you may find yourself rubbing shoulders with past professionals who can still turn a wheel well, but will also be more than willing to offer you advice and help as you race.

Whichever kind of racing you decide to start with, we will demonstrate how you can plan, train and race as successfully as possible and gain the maximum amount of enjoyment out of what is an exciting and rewarding sport. By using tried and tested training methods and introducing you to the relevant skills and techniques, we can help you to become a racing cyclist.

CHAPTER 2
Equipment and Set-Up

Although the rider is the most important element in cycling sport, there is undoubtedly a significant reliance upon equipment. A top-quality bike will not make a great rider better, but a good bike will help any rider reach their potential, as the bike plays a major part in transferring the skill, fitness and talent of the rider into results. For a bicycle to perform well in a competitive environment and give its rider the confidence to perform to their best, it must fit well and be mechanically sound. There are some components that will help the rider to perform better and we will discuss these as we work through the mechanics of a bicycle. We will also help you to find a bike that fits and will ensure that your bike is adjusted correctly to make you as efficient as possible.

Frames

Frames have progressed hugely in recent years. Twenty years ago, every racing bike was made of steel tubing welded into place and then painted to the manufacturer's, customer's or sponsor's requirements. Frames are now available in steel, aluminium, titanium, carbon

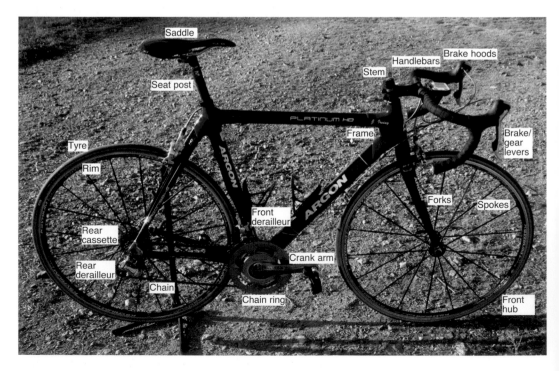

The components of a bicycle.

A standard road bike handlebar set-up.

fibre, or any mixture of these. Frame designs have also altered significantly, with the introduction of compact frames in any material. These alterations in frame materials and sizing have made it more difficult to prescribe a frame size. With the traditional frame design it was possible to work out the desired frame size in inches or centimetres from the rider's inside-leg measurements. With the current design innovations and an increase in the number of frames imported from different parts of the world, where measurements are taken from different parts of the frame, this calculation is no longer valid and once again it comes down to developing a relationship with a good local bicycle dealer or using the calculations we will detail later in this chapter, then setting out to find a frame that accommodates your required dimensions as opposed to the other way around. A closer look at the components of a bicycle will help us to identify the variances available.

Handlebars

The two types of handlebars shown in the illustrations are those commonly used for competitive road cycling. The road handlebars allow the rider a wide variety of positions, thus reducing fatigue while allowing access to the brakes and gear selection system. There is not a great deal of variety with handlebars. although they do need to be the correct size for the rider so as to ensure they are both comfortable and safe. The correct size is a match for the width of the shoulders of the rider.

There is a wide variety of styles and designs for the aerodynamic bars that are widely referred to as tri-bars. Borrowed from the then emerging sport of Triathlon, the American cyclist Greg Lemond rode to victory in the 1989 Tour de France using these bars and from then on they were the way for riders to get lower and narrower and therefore more aerodynamic and faster. The designs have developed, but the basic principle of lowering the rider onto a pair of narrow bars and at the front bringing the arms together, therefore reducing the frontal area of resistance, has been consistent. Tri-bars can be bought to attach to standard road bars. This is a great way of using one bike for both road racing and time trials and is a very common sight. The principles

A time trial bike set-up with specific bars and tri-bars. Bar end gear selectors and specific brake levers can also be seen.

remain the same as the overall height of the rider is reduced as is the frontal area. More specialized time trial bikes have bars similar to that in the photograph, but again there will be a wide variance in style on view at any local time trial race in the UK. When sizing tri-bars the extension is important, and whilst this is normally adjustable, the principles discussed in the cycle fit section (*see* below) will apply.

Braking Systems

The components of the braking system are the brake lever, the brake cable and the brake caliper. The right-hand brake lever normally operates the front brake and the left-hand lever the rear brake. It is important that you

know which lever operates which brake so that you can use the ratios and braking practices we will discuss later. There is little variance in brake lever type and on standard road bikes (as illustrated) the location of the lever can be adjusted slightly on the front curve of the bar to ensure that the lever can be reached and operated safely. The lever pictured also houses the gear selector. Some tri-bars have different types of levers, although their method of operation is the same. They are not adjustable in position, but are easily accessible.

The brake calipers work by having a number of parts, which, when pulled together, squeeze the brake pads onto the rim. The brake pads are therefore a very important part of the system and must be in

A standard road bike brake lever. This also includes the gear selection lever on the inside of the brake lever.

A road bike brake lever. This design has been around for some time and works well, in addition to looking good.

good order with plenty of material on them. Most wheels are aluminium and will work well with the pads that are supplied as standard with the bike or calipers, but if you are fortunate enough to have wheels that have carbon fibre as a braking surface you will need specific brake pads designed to operate on this surface.

The brake cables should also receive attention – as the component that transfers the action from the rider through the lever to the caliper they must be in good working order. Cables have improved a lot over recent decades, with the development of low-resistance inner and outer cables that have already been stretched, meaning that they can be a fit-and-forget item. They will need replacing every so often to ensure they remain an efficient part of the system.

Chain Sets and Pedals

Chain sets on road race and time trial bikes will normally have two chain rings. There is no reason why a rider can't race with a triple chain set, but there is obviously going to be a minor weight penalty. The chain rings are often described by their size, with the smaller chain ring generally being between thirty-nine and forty-two teeth and the larger chain ring being between forty-nine and fifty-four, with fifty-two as virtually the industry standard. The size of the chain rings combined with the size of the rear sprockets (a sprocket is a profiled wheel with teeth) and the circumference of the wheel makes the gear ratio. Riders will often simply refer to their gear by its tooth size, for example: a fifty-two by thirteen refers to a gear that has a chain ring size of fifty-two and a sprocket size of thirteen. The larger the difference between the chain ring size and the sprocket size, the larger the gear and therefore the further you will travel with every pedal revolution. The gears on your bike will help you to ride and race effectively. A hilly race will require a wider range of gears than a flat event. Steep climbs will need smaller gears

The location of the brake levers on a specific time trial bike with specialist handlebars.

A standard road or time trial bike chain set.

that are easier to push, such as would be achieved with a chain set size of thirty-nine and a rear sprocket of twenty-two. Establishing a balance between the gears that your bike has and the gears that you need to suit your abilities will take a little time, but this should be achieved by experimenting during training.

There is some variance in chain set type other than number and size of chain rings. The material the chain set is made of will have an impact upon its weight and this is often a factor when putting a bike together. There is some variance in the length of the cranks (the arms that attach the chain rings to the pedals), with some experienced riders preferring a longer crank to give them greater leverage. Generally, the cranks supplied are 170mm long and for the vast majority of riders and events this will be perfectly suitable.

One of the recent advances in bicycle design has been the introduction of clipless pedals. This term refers to pedals that do not have the traditional toe clip that was common up until the late 1980s. Bernard Hinault was one of the first high-profile riders to start using a clipless system, which was originally based upon the system used for skis. There are now many clipless systems available and advice on suitability for any specific rider is best given by your local independent bicycle dealer. The systems are broadly similar, with a fixing or cleat attached to the bottom of the cycling shoe, which, when pressed onto the pedal, will click into place. Once in place, the shoe will be securely fixed and only a small amount of movement will be possible until the rider wants to take the shoe off the pedal, when a twist to the side will free the shoe from the pedal.

The rear gear mechanism pictured with gear sprockets on the rear cassette.

The front gear mechanism in position over the chain set.

Gears

A racing bicycle will normally have a gear mechanism on the chain set called the front mech and on the rear sprockets called the rear mech. Operated by cables from gear levers which are commonly found on handlebars (*see* photograph above of a brake lever), the gears move the chain across the sprockets and chain rings to vary the gear available to the rider. Gear levers can also be found on the down tube, a location that was the norm until the late 1990s, and with time trial bikes they can often be found at the end of the tri-bars (*see* the tri-bar photograph). The two major manufacturers of gear systems are Shimano and Campagnolo and both types are used in equal measure by professional cyclists and amateurs alike. The choice is often personal and may just come down to aesthetics, although there are some operational differences between the two. Both manufacturers have a wide range of component ranges, referred to as group sets, to enable a rider to find a group set that meets their needs, preferences and pocket.

The gear mechanisms themselves vary little among the manufacturers, although some material differences are available, with an increased use of carbon fibre for both aesthetic purposes and weight reduction. As with the braking system, the cables must be in a good state of repair and are crucial to the precise operation of the gear systems, which must be correctly adjusted to ensure that the gear you select is the one to which the mechanism shifts the chain and then keeps the chain in the correct place. Poor condition or maintenance can lead to sloppy changes or jumping between gears, both of which need to be avoided to make your training enjoyable and your racing competitive. The number of sprockets on the rear cassette has steadily increased over the past twenty years, to the point that most bikes now have nine or ten sprockets on the rear cassette. This gives the rider a wide selection of gears and removes the need to select different sprockets and change them to suit the kind of racing.

Wheels

There are a huge number of different wheels available to the racing cyclist, with many entry level racing bikes being supplied from the outset with good-quality wheels. Years ago, all racing wheels were hand-built by highly skilled wheel builders who would use the hub and rim of your selection and lace them using high-quality spokes. This practice has been altered significantly by the introduction of high-quality, very durable and light machine-built wheels. Many spokes are now flattened to be more aerodynamic and the method of lacing has also changed in many instances. Rim technology has also moved on, with carbon fibre being used in preference to aluminium so as to produce lighter, more aerodynamic wheels, often with deeper rims. These wheels are great for time trialling and can also be used in road racing, but are more susceptible to side winds and can be difficult to handle in a group situation when it is breezy. Selection of wheels is again a personal matter, with aesthetics and budget being the most important factors You will see a wide variety of wheel designs at most races and a quick chat with the users will give you an idea of the advantages and disadvantages of differing designs.

A standard mid-range road race wheel.

An aerodynamic deep-rimmed carbon-fibre wheel.

THE BICYCLE SET-UP

Now that we understand the components of a bicycle, we can focus on establishing the correct riding position. The three areas that need to be considered are safety, comfort and efficiency. As we are concentrating on cycling for sport with the aim of achieving maximum performance, efficiency is the most important of the three areas. This does not mean that safety and comfort will be ignored, but some minor compromises will be necessary in order to achieve the most efficient and fast position. This is probably best demonstrated by the position adopted for time trialling, in which the rider cannot easily access the brake levers or indeed change position without significant body movement. The traditional road race position is probably less of a compromise, but it is still less comfortable and arguably less safe than the position adopted when on a standard bike.

When working on cycle position, we need to look at the points of contact, which include the pedals, the saddle and the handlebars. To follow this logically, we will start with the pedals and then move up and forwards.

As the principal point of power transfer, the pedal is arguably the most important point of contact with the bike. Much of the set-up in this area, when using clipless pedals, will refer to the adjustment of the cleat on the bottom of the shoe. First of all, it is vital that your cycling shoes are a good fit. Providing this is the case, the cleat needs to be set up to ensure that the ball of the foot is directly over the axle of the pedal. This position will ensure that, with a good cycling shoe, all of the power will flow through the pedal as efficiently as possible. This position will also help to prevent injuries to the knee, which can be caused by poorly adjusted cleats. Once in place, the foot should feel comfortable without any tension on the knee. If you feel that the knee is being twisted, alter the cleat very slightly. Adjustments in this area should only be very small. It may take a bit of trial and error to establish the right position for you, but so long as the basic principle of the ball of the foot over the axle is maintained you will have the starting point for a good, effective position.

Moving upwards, we concentrate next on the height of the saddle, which is measured from the top of the pedal axle to the top of the saddle. This allows for variance in saddle type, but will provide a measure that can be applied to any bicycle you may ride.

The basic formula for establishing the distance from the pedal axle to the top of the saddle is:

- Inseam × 1.09 (+/- 0.3, i.e. 1.06–1.12). Where inseam is taken as the inside leg measurement from the floor to the groin.

Apply this to an inseam of 82cm:

- 82 × 1.06 = 86.92
- 82 × 1.09 = 89.38
- 82 × 1.12 = 91.84.

Start with the centre figure of the range and set this as the saddle height, then try the bike for size wearing your cycling shorts and shoes. When the leg is in place, it should be almost but not entirely straight. If you have been riding extensively prior to carrying out these measurements, any adjustment you make should be minor. If there is a great deal of adjustment to be made to achieve the position we are prescribing, the changes should be gradual and certainly no more than half a centimetre per week.

Once the correct position for the height of the saddle has been established, you will need to look at the lateral adjustment and the tilt of the saddle. With saddle tilt, it is best to start the process with a saddle that is effectively flat. This can then be adjusted to find a more comfortable position. Many women find a slight downwards tilt more comfortable, but this should only be slight. Experimentation is the key to achieving a long-term comfortable set-up.

The lateral adjustment of the saddle is a little more prescriptive, as this has a direct impact on the efficiency of the pedalling action. The saddle should be laterally adjusted so that when normally seated and with the pedal at three o'clock, the rider's knee is almost over the pedal axle.

The ball of the foot should be over the axle to ensure a good transfer of power.

If substantial adjustment of the lateral position of the saddle is required to achieve this, a further check of the saddle height must be completed to ensure this measurement is still accurate and relevant.

The handlebars should be in such a position that the rider can reach the brake levers safely without having to adopt an upright, and therefore non-aerodynamic, position. This can be achieved by altering the height of the handlebars by inserting or removing spacers at the top of the handlebars and by changing the length of the stem. Adjusting the position of the handlebars will not compensate for a frame that is either too large or too small, which could result in a bike that is dangerous to ride due to unpredictable handling.

Setting up tri-bars is an added complication and here the main objective is to get low and reduce the frontal area, although the position should not be compromised as power output and subsequently speed will suffer. Therefore, once you have estab-lished the correct position for the saddle regarding height and lateral movement, the handlebars and tri-bars should be set up to achieve the best aerodynamic and low position. Achieving the optimum position will maintain your efficiency and improve your drag.

RACING BIKES FOR FEMALES

There are differences in the way that women and men are proportioned. On average, women cyclists have longer legs and shorter torsos relative to their overall height. Much of this 'extra length' comes from the thigh bone, which then makes up a higher percentage of leg length in women than in men. This is especially true in taller women, who form the majority of the female elite triath-lete and cycling population. Women are also on average shorter than men. More importantly, women have narrower shoulders and smaller feet and hands.

OPPOSITE: The knee over the pedal axle.

ABOVE: The relationship between the position of the rider and the handlebars.

But what does this mean for bike design and set-up? Traditionally, bikes were sized up simply according to inside leg length or 'stand-over height' (and in many shops they sadly still are). However, for most women this will lead to too big a frame, given their proportionally longer legs relative to height and in particular torso length. The unsuspecting woman is usually then sold a short stem and a straight seat pin – most seat pins slope backwards slightly to get the most legs in the optimum position for adding power to the pedal stroke – in order to shorten the distance between the saddle and the handlebars. This is a highly unsatisfactory compromise. The handling of the bike will be affected and the position of the knees relative to the feet (too far forwards) will cause poor power transfer and, probably, sore knees. All in all, an uncomfortable and unresponsive ride.

Current recommendations for sizing bicycles are more focused on top-tube length, so many women are simply sold a smaller frame size in order to get the correct top-tube length. But this in itself is only half the problem. Stem length and saddle position still need to be optimized. Also, there may not always be a smaller size frame available!

There are an increasing number of cycle manufacturers looking to cash in on the expansion in the marketplace by offering female-specific road bikes and other equipment. 'Women's specific geometry' is promoted as, in the main, a shorter top tube and smaller frame sizes. Whilst the latter is undoubtedly very helpful, the former may or may not be the answer: it depends on how this is achieved. The simplest and cheapest way to achieve a shorter bike top tube is to bring the seat tube forwards to bring the saddle closer to the handlebars. In practice, this usually means making the seat tube more upright – steeper.

In order for maximum transmission of the power from the contraction of the thigh muscles to the pedals the foot and knee must be properly aligned over the pedal spindle. Sitting too far forwards or back will result in inefficient power transmission and also risk knee pain. As mentioned earlier,

women tend to have relatively longer legs and in particular the thigh bone. Thus to achieve an optimal knee/foot/pedal position, that rider will need to sit well behind the bottom-bracket area. In those designs where the top tube is created by steepening the seat tube, the opposite happens. So, our rider moves the saddle as far back as it will go. The reach is now again too long, so she buys a shorter handlebar stem and we are back to square one.

A truly female-specific frame can therefore only be achieved by redesigning the whole geometry to create a shorter top tube and a shallower seat-tube angle. The leaders in this field are the American Bicycle Group, designers and manufacturers of Quintano Roo, Merlin and Litespeed. The company has not only invested in a full geometrical redesign for its frames but also for a range of forks which give excellent race bike handling qualities even on smaller bikes.

Female-Specific Components and Accessories

Finally, we come to the array of female-specific components and accessories: which of these do we really need? Yes, narrower width bars will help to optimize the riding position, make it more aerodynamic (smaller frontal area) and also take some of the strain off the shoulders, but these bars also need to be shorter front to back. Shimano Ultegra shifter levers are available with an inset wedge to fit smaller hands and the new Dura Ace ones are shaped so that the risk of putting on the brakes whilst shifting gear is minimized. However, in general, Campagnolo levers offer a better grip for smaller hands and are easier to operate from the brake hoods. Most women seem to prefer riding on the brake hoods to the drop-bar bends. This has often been assumed to be due to shorter reach (*see* the raised handlebar issue above), but in fact it is undoubtedly due to smaller hands feeling more secure whilst braking from this position compared with fingertip only contact from the drops. Crank and stem length need to be proportional to the bike and the rider not used as a way of adapting the bike to fit. A smaller woman with small feet will benefit from shorter cranks – not for ease of spinning, as the lighter muscles will aid that anyway, but simply to make the bike fit her!

And the Saddle ...

So last, but not least, the saddle – yes, of course this is the area where women are most different to men, but to look at many of the 'women's saddles' you would think that all women have huge posteriors! Wider hips don't require wider saddles; indeed, most women's hip measurements are smaller than those of men. When riding in a race position, the weight is borne not by the pelvic bones but further forwards, more so in men due to the forward rotation of the pelvis.

Therefore, the ideal women's racing saddle should be long and not too wide at the back, to facilitate being able to move backwards in order to get power from the thighs, but also soft and slightly tilted down at the front so as to alleviate pressure in this region. With such an array of different saddles available on the market, there ought to be one that suits each woman's shape and riding style some-where ... shouldn't there?

We have looked in some detail at the wide variety of equipment available to the racing cyclist, considered some of the advantages and disadvantages of different equipment and made some recommendations regarding sourcing racing equipment. We have also looked at how to set up your racing bike to get the most out of it and be as efficient as possible. You are now in a strong position to start training and racing.

CHAPTER 3
Basic Skills

Cycling is a sport which requires a great deal of physical ability, but also the development of specific skills for both training and racing. In this chapter, we will examine these skills and how we can develop our abilities. We will do this by breaking down each skill, looking at the requirements for basic riding and training and then studying how the skill is developed for the purposes of racing. We will also explain any race specific-skills wherever appropriate.

STARTING

The basic technique of safe starting is to stand with the bicycle next to the kerb, pointing in the direction of travel. Place both hands on the top of the handlebars. Look over your right shoulder to check for traffic, then swing the right leg over the saddle and place it on the pedal, which should be at two o'clock. Move your bottom onto the saddle and then prepare to push down on the pedal

ABOVE: *Ready for the off!*

OPPOSITE: *The traditional time trial start.*

and move off, checking over the right shoulder just before doing so to ensure that the road is still clear of passing traffic. Once moving, bring the left leg onto the pedal and continue to pedal. This process is easiest when using a kerb to balance on, but you should also be able to do it without a kerb. Using clipless pedals will make this action a little more complicated, but you need to become competent at getting the pedals clipped in as quickly as possible so that you can pedal forwards without loosing momentum. This can be helped by ensuring that the gear you move off in is suitable, neither too hard (high) or too easy (low). The correct gear will enable you to push off with a little effort and give you enough momentum from the initial revolution, so that you have time to get your other foot clipped in.

The technique for road racing starts is not very different. Most road races start with all riders seated on bikes, then moving off together. This means that all riders will have to go through the process of clipping in, thus a road race starts with a succession of clicks as between fifty and eighty riders place their feet into the pedals. Road races are often 'neutralized' for the first section of the race. This means that the race has a slow start and riders are given the opportunity to get their feet in the right place and get the feel of the bike before the racing starts. The start of the race is often indicated by the lead car withdrawing a red flag, or in a circuit race the first lap will often be neutralized, with a union flag waved to indicate the start of racing. This is worth checking, as some races start from the gun, meaning that a quick action and good gear selection become very important.

Time trial starts are very different. To give the rider the best possible chance of getting a good start and performing well, almost all time trials start with the rider being held. In principle, this simply involves going through the same process as if you were moving off on your own, but at this point the holder will take the bicycle by the seat pin and the headset in order to hold you in position prior to the starter counting you down to head off. You will normally only be held for the last thirty seconds, although it may feel like a lot longer. You will probably feel as if you are leaning slightly. A good holder will hold you as upright as possible, but may need some direction as to your optimal starting position. Gear selection in this instance is very important, as the gear that you set off in will need to be the best one to suit the conditions and the terrain over the first few metres.

BRAKING

Having started off, we need to feel confident that we can slow down and stop. The brakes will be operated by the levers on the bars. It is worth checking which lever operates which brake, as the balance between the front and back brake is crucial when operating the brakes at speed. Most UK bikes have the front brake operated by the lever on the right-hand side of the bars, but this may not be the case with the bike you are riding, so it is essential to establish which brake is which. When braking to slow down on dry roads, the emphasis should be slightly on the rear brake, so as to avoid the rear wheel locking up and a skid occurring. However, the front brake also needs to be used to balance the braking power. When you are coming to a halt, the front brake needs to be used more – a 60 per cent preference for the front brake should deliver the necessary power. Wet surfaces or those roads with unstable surfaces require a greater degree of caution and braking should be a lot more progressive to avoid skidding. Careful practice is required to build up confidence in knowing when and where to brake. The last thing you want to do is loose speed and momentum that you have spent a long time gaining.

In a racing scenario, the efficiency of braking is even more important. In time trialling, the use of brakes should be limited, unless the course is technical in nature. Even so, you need to practise braking in training to ensure that you know when and how to brake in order to maintain your speed and be safe. You should not brake when cornering or leaning – as with motoring, braking should be done when going straight and level. As in top motor sports driving, skilful application of the brakes into and through corners can be combined effectively, but this is definitely not a skill for novices! In road racing, there is a much greater requirement for safe and efficient braking. We will discuss some aspects of this in the group riding section, but essentially you need to be able to brake to control your speed when manoeuvring around corners and obstacles. Being smooth and not losing speed unnecessarily is vitally important and while races are not won in corners, they can certainly be lost there.

CORNERING

You will, at some point very soon in your cycling career, need to go around a corner. The process of cornering is not difficult, but in our context we want to be able to corner at speed. In order to achieve this, we need to combine the braking skills detailed above with some additional techniques. There are a number of considerations to take into account when looking at any given cornering situation. The cornering technique may also be applied when you need to manoeuvre around an obstacle in the road or follow the best line for time trialling. In road racing, the demands of concerning and your ability to influence the line may be restricted, but the principals are the same. Your key considerations are:

- surface
- entry speed
- exit speed
- fastest line
- tyre condition.

Your overall objective for any corner in a racing situation is to get through it as fast as you can, while losing as little speed as

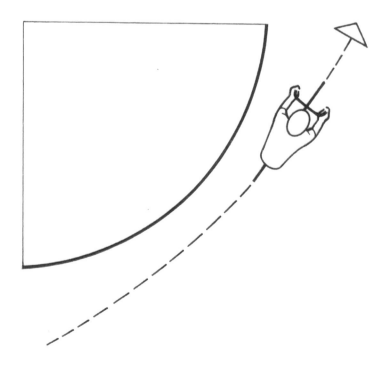

ABOVE: The racing line through a corner.

Coming off the tri-bars to apply the brakes is a specific time trialling skill.

ABOVE: *Selecting the right gear for an attack out of the saddle is vital.*

OVERLEAF: *A group riding closely together during a race.*

possible. There is a route through the corner that is often referred to as the line. When riding alone on roads that are free of traffic, you can use the perfect line, that is, the straightest line around any given corner or bend. This involves the process of straightening out the bend (*see* diagram below).

As the rider approaches the corner, they move to the left-hand side of the road. They then envisage the line through the corner, look towards it and start the turning process. By ensuring that the inside pedal is up, most of the cornering will be achieved through leaning. Once the centre, or apex, of the corner is reached,

the rider will start to head towards the exit, at which point they will be almost fully upright and ready to accelerate.

The body position is very important when cornering, as the distribution of weight will affect the handling of the bike through the bend. It is best to hold the bars at the lowest point and the rider must remain seated throughout the turn. Once in the corner, the pedal nearest to the inside of the corner must be at the top of its revolution. The knees should remain pointing forwards and the elbows should remain in, although the shoulder can be dropped slightly to put weight in towards the centre of the corner. Weight should be

Using power to good effect in an uphill attack.

lifted very slightly off the saddle and onto the outside pedal, which will also aid with correct positioning of the body.

Cornering can make the difference between a successful race or an average result. In time trials, there is an increased use of circular courses that test the rider's technical abilities. Such courses involve a lot of cornering and so the ability to corner quickly will be vital. In road racing, you will need to develop your ability to corner and then apply this to a bunch situation. This will require a great deal of trust, but will result in a much more efficient race.

You will need to find a venue that allows you to practise your cornering; alternatively, you could build a small training route which involves a lot of cornering. Cornering must become second nature, to the point where you can judge the appropriate speed for a corner without pushing so hard that you become acquainted with the tarmac. This will only be achieved through constant practice.

CHANGING GEAR

This section will outline the basic skill of changing gear. The purpose of changing gears is to allow you to use your body as efficiently as possible. Efficiency is achieved by pedalling at the correct speed. This is referred to as cadence and is measured in the number of revolutions per minute of the rider's feet in the pedals. It is generally accepted that the optimum cadence for performance is between 80 and 100 revolutions per minute. This is quite a wide range, but it does provide enough flexibility to accommodate different riding styles. The current fashion is for a brisker cadence, which is achieved by pushing in a lower gear. Gears are generally called 'high' or 'low', referring to the distance travelled for any given revolution. A lower gear travels a lower distance per revolution than a higher gear. A gear that is easy to push around is very low, while a gear that is hard to push is high. Most bikes now have between fourteen and twenty gears and will have a gear selector on

the rear cogs and a mechanism on the front chain ring or chain set (where the pedals are attached) in order to move between the gears. The rear cogs are called sprockets and the gear, which is defined as a ratio, is a combination of the size of the rear sprockets, counted in teeth, and the size of the chain rings, also counted in teeth. The greater the difference between the number of teeth on the sprockets and chain ring, the higher the gear will be and the further you will travel with each pedal revolution.

There are generally two chain rings at the front controlled by the gear selector on the left-hand side of the bike (*see* the equipment section in Chapter 2) and there will be between seven and ten sprockets on the rear of the bike controlled by the gear selector on the right-hand side of the bike. Minor changes in gear are achieved by using the rear selector controlled by the right-hand lever and major changes are achieved by shifting chain rings using the left-hand selector. Most races, other than very hilly races, will require the large chain ring to be used almost exclusively with adjustments to accommodate terrain or pace made using the rear sprockets and rear mechanism controlled by the right-hand lever.

Gears should be used to make the bike and rider as efficient as possible, usually by using the gears to maintain a cadence of between eighty to one hundred revolutions per minute. A cycle computer fixed to your bike will indicate the cadence you are achieving. Alternatively, a count over a set period (fifteen or thirty seconds is best) will give you a pretty good idea. You will then get a feel for your natural cadence and understand what needs to be done to increase this into an efficient zone. This may feel unnatural, but will pay dividends in the long run.

A well-adjusted bike will, once directed by the lever, change gears quite efficiently. A slight easing in the pressure applied to the pedals will assist the chain while it is moving through this process, although it is more important when moving to a lower gear (changing down) than when moving to a higher gear (changing up). Anticipation is often a better tactic and by assessing what gear is required in advance, you will be able to set up the bike and adjust your cadence as required.

Many entry level road bikes will have the range of gears required to accommodate racing, but if you are riding especially hilly or very fast flat events you may want to consider looking at the gears available to you. Similarly, should you discover that you have a talent for sprinting at the end of a road race, the range of gears on your bike may also need to be considered. A higher top gear will allow you to sprint or pedal at a lower cadence for a given speed, but it may require too much effort to push to be economical for somebody who naturally pedals at a higher cadence.

The jump between gears is also a consideration and in flat time trials and many road races subtle adjustments are all that is required to maintain economy of effort. To help with this, a rear set of sprockets with very small changes in size between adjacent sprockets, often referred to as block, could be fitted. Changing to this set of sprockets is not a difficult job, but for the novice the assistance of a local cycle shop would be the best option as the people there will be able to help with compatibility of parts.

CLIMBING

Regardless of where about you live, you will, at some point, come across a climb. This may only be a slight rise along a major road or motorway, or it could be a 10km drag to the top of an alpine pass. There will obviously be a significant difference in your approach to these two ascents. In order to be successful in climbs, you will need to be aware of your physical and mental ability and limitations. Road races in particular can be won and lost in hilly terrain. Gear selection is vital for climbing and it is important to have the right gears on your bike for a particular race.

Short climbs use a different energy system in the body to longer climbs as they are essentially uphill sprints. A bigger rider is likely to be able to produce more power than a smaller rider, and on a short climb this power can be used to get the rider to the top more quickly. On a longer climb, however, the lighter rider who produces less power will be more effective as they may have a better power-to-weight ratio, so even through they produce less power overall they are more powerful when gravity has a greater role to play, as it does on long climbs. The power to weight ratio will become more important on longer climbs and a degree of pacing will be required to ensure that you get to the top. In a time trial, the pacing is important but it is up to the individual. In a road race environment, you need to stay in contact with the group in order to stand a chance of succeeding in the race. This will impact upon your pacing of a climb, but your position within the group can help you. By moving towards the front of the group at the bottom of the climb you will be allowing yourself some degree of space to slip back through the group as other riders climb at a better pace. This kind of tactic will work on shorter to medium length hills, but on the longer climbs if you are not able to keep up with the pack's climbing pace you will eventually find yourself on your own.

Body weight is an obvious factor affecting climbing ability, so by reducing this and increasing power output (how hard you can pedal), you will climb faster. It may be that your natural physique does not lend itself to climbing quickly; for example, a rider over 183cm (6ft) tall will struggle to reduce their weight to the same level as a rider just over 152cm (5ft). The best practice is to go out and ride hills. By training hard and eating well, your weight will reduce and your power will increase. Training with friends will help, as they will ride at different paces, which will help you to push yourself.

GROUP RIDING

The ability to ride with other people is important for all competitive cyclists. The reason is obvious for the road racer but time triallists may want to training with other people, and they will defiantly get a benefit out of it, and they may also want to take part in team time trials of either two three or four people. While this is s smaller group it still requires the same skills.

Within a road race, if you are not confident and competent at riding with other people you will find the experience uncomfortable and considerably harder work. The basic skill of riding with other people is known as 'following a wheel'. This is the phrase used to describe riding closely behind another rider. The advantages are the slipstreaming effect – the rider in front passes thorough the air first and so reduces the resistance presented to the rider behind. It is estimated that the effort required by the rider behind is reduced by up to 30 per cent. This kind of saving is really beneficial and is essential in maintaining speed in the group. Staying away from the front of the pack will help you to complete your first road race.

The ability to ride closely side by side is also important, as you will loose valuable places if you are not confident in holding a position within the pack as people squeeze alongside you through the course of the race. This kind of ability can only be practised within a group, for example by riding with a good cycling club, although your first race will feel much more compact than the average club ride. Gear selection when cornering and braking will become even more important, as you will be aiming to be a smooth part of the group without wasting any energy.

We have listed some of the skills required, but the real key to becoming a competent rider lies in combining these skills during a competitive session and learning when a particular skill is required. This will become instinctive at some point, but it may take a while to do so.

CHAPTER 4

The Science Behind Basic Sports Nutrition and Cycle Training

Cycling is one of the sports that has benefited most from sport science, mainly because the majority of sport-science research involves, at some point or other, a volunteer on an exercise bicycle. From these origins, more in-depth and complex research has looked at how best to optimize training and bike set-up to get the most out of the human body. Whilst sport science itself can be a complex subject requiring a good knowledge of anatomy and medical physiology, a basic understanding of its principles can help a rider to appreciate the reasoning behind training methods and sports nutrition and thus prepare better for an event. There are three key areas:

• heart, circulation and breathing
• muscles and nerves
• aerobic and anaerobic systems.

HEART, CIRCULATION AND BREATHING

The heart, along with the brain, is the key organ within the human body and quite literally the source of life itself. The heart is, in fact, a special type of muscle, one that needs to keep contracting and relaxing, from before we are born throughout the whole of our lives. The heart is at the centre of the circulatory system, which also includes all the blood and the blood vessels, the arteries and

veins. The heart pumps the blood round the body through a system of arteries leading to the muscles and other organs, with the system of veins returning the blood back to the heart to be recirculated via the lungs and then back around the body again.

The blood delivers vital oxygen, along with dissolved nutrients, to the working muscles (*see* below) and other organs and carries away waste products. Oxygen is carried within the blood tagged onto the red blood cells. Put simply, muscle cells have a greater affinity for oxygen than the red blood cells, so the oxygen molecules are given up by the blood cells and absorbed into the muscle cells. The now oxygen-depleted blood returns to the heart and is pumped to the tissues deep within the lungs, where new oxygen molecules are absorbed into the red blood cells. The oxygen-rich blood is then returned to the heart, whereupon it is recirculated to the muscles once again.

As we will see later, the gas carbon dioxide is a waste product of muscle activity and this is transferred from the muscles into the bloodstream, then returned via the heart to the lungs, where it diffuses out of the bloodstream into the lungs themselves and is breathed out. Thus breathing is simply a matter of renewing the oxygen supply to the blood and expelling the waste carbon dioxide.

The rate of supply of oxygen and the removal of carbon dioxide are critical to the rate at which a muscle can work. The more

Climbing out of the saddle can really get the heart rate up.

active a muscle is, the more oxygen it requires and the more carbon dioxide needs to be transported away. The same is true of the nutritional fuels that the muscle requires, which are also transported via the bloodstream.

The rate of supply of blood to a muscle is governed by two different factors:
• the rate at which the heart beats, or your pulse, measured in beats per minute (bpm)
• the amount of blood pumped round the body per beat, measured in millilitres. (known as stroke volume).
The combined effect of these two factors is known as the 'cardiac output', that is, the amount of blood per minute pumped by the heart, which is measured as millilitres of blood per minute:
• cardiac output = pulse rate _ stroke volume (millilitres per min) (beats per min) (millilitres per beat).

One well-known consequence of regular exercise is that the resting heart rate drops, as does the heart rate at any given exercise rate. This is because the heart muscle itself responds to training just like other muscle and is able to do its job more efficiently. It does this by contracting more forcefully and therefore increases the amount of blood pumped per beat (that is, the stroke volume increases). At a given activity level, the body requires a certain amount of blood (that is, a certain cardiac output), so given that the stroke volume has increased, the pulse rate can decrease with the same net result.

Of course, when you exercise – regardless of how fit you are – the heart rate goes up. This is because the working muscles require more fuel and oxygen and more waste product needs to be transported away. When you first start training, you find the pulse rate jumps up very quickly, but as you get fitter this rate of increase is less marked and you can sustain your work rate for longer. This is because the heart muscle has become stronger and so can increase stroke volume as well as pulse rate to fulfil the extra demands.

As already noted, the heart muscle responds to training just like any other muscle. The heart is comprised of two elements – the pumping chambers through which the blood to be pumped flows and the thick muscular walls which do the pumping. It is the contracting of these muscles forcing the blood through the pumping chambers that causes the lub-dub heart sound you can hear with a stethoscope.

Just like any other muscle, the heart muscle fibres require oxygen and nutritional fuel in order to do their job. With regular exercise, the fibres adapt and become more efficient and their own blood supply increases in much the same way as with other muscles, as we will learn later. So a regularly exercised heart is a healthy and efficient heart with a lower resting pulse rate and greater stroke volume.

Maximal heart rate – the highest pulse rate an individual can attain – depends very much on age and genetics, but essentially is fixed regardless of training. So increasing the amount of blood circulated per beat is critically important to sports performance, especially as most training and racing is done well below maximal heart rate.

When you start to exercise, not only does the heart rate increase but so does the breathing rate. Just like heart rate, there are two key factors – the amount of breath inhaled and exhaled per breath and the number of breaths per minute. With regular exercise, the muscles involved in breathing – including the intercostal (rib) muscles and the diaphragm – become stronger. The amount of breath inhaled and exhaled therefore increases, with the result that the rate of breathing at any given exercise level drops. The familiar excuse among unfit people running for a bus is that they are 'out of breath'. This really is a misnomer, as it is very unlikely that we can ever stretch our respiratory (breathing) system to this level, but is more an expression of the discomfort experienced by working untrained breathing muscles.

Carbon dioxide is one of the main products of exercise activity and is transported from the working muscles to the lungs for exhalation via the bloodstream. Sensors in the bloodstream detect the increase in carbon dioxide that is created by an increase in muscle activity and so stimulate the breathing mechanisms to make us breathe deeper and faster. This, in turns, gets rid of the excess carbon dioxide and provides a greater supply of oxygen. The breathing rate is thereby controlled via a supply-and-demand type of mechanism.

Finally, there are changes within the circulatory system – those arteries and veins that transport oxygen, fuel, carbon dioxide and other waste products around the body – and these are some of the most significant changes that happen with training.

To explain, we need to look at bit more closely at the mechanics. The main artery leaving the heart (the aorta) is quite thick and wide – about the thickness of a thumb. This divides into smaller arteries and these again into even smaller arterioles as the blood supply tubes reach the muscles and other organs. Although very small, the walls of these tubes are still too thick for the fuel and oxygen to diffuse through. For this to happen, the arterioles are further divided into a network of microscopically fine capillaries. The thickness of a hair and with a wall only one cell thick, these capillaries permeate deep into the muscle tissue, allowing oxygen to be delivered throughout the body of the muscle. In summary:

• heart ➤ aorta ➤ arteries ➤ arterioles ➤ capillaries ➤ venules ➤ veins ➤ heart.

With regular exercise this capillary network grows, taking blood deeper within the muscle tissue so that more and more muscle fibres are directly receiving oxygen and fuel-carrying blood. The more oxygen and fuel the muscle fibres receive, the more activity they can do with less fatigue, especially as this same network will carry away a greater amount of waste product. Regular exercise increases the amount of oxygenated blood that reaches the muscles, thereby enhancing the muscle's capacity to do 'work'.

MUSCLES AND NERVES

Cycle training clearly involves the leg muscles, but what changes take place as a result of training? How does training make the muscles fitter and what exactly is that fitness?

You only have to look at an elite cyclist's body to see the effect of training on muscle mass and definition. Likewise, you can also see the different types and builds of riders – big, strong muscles are clearly an advantage in a sprint, but a lithe, lean body is better for climbing. Which camp you fall into depends on a number of factors – your genetic body type, your training regime and your diet.

Basically, body type falls into three categories – although most of us are a combination of two types:

- **ectomorph:** long bones, often tall and with a predisposition to leanness – the proverbial stick-insect type that no amount of gym work will turn into a Mr or Mrs Universe
- **mesomorph:** broad shoulders, narrow waisted and heavily muscled – only has to look at a dumbbell for the muscles to grow
- **endomorph:** more rounded with a propensity for putting on weight.

Ectomorph types tend to be better suited to climbing and endurance activities, whilst mesomorphs tend to be better suited to shorter sprint activities. Endomorphs can fall into either camp, depending mainly on diet and training. Knowing which category you belong to can help to inform your choice of cycling activity, although it is important to remember that this is only a guide and there may examples of exceptions to these 'rules'.

Perhaps the most important genetic factor in sport is your muscle type. Broadly speaking, there are two types of muscle fibre:

- **slow twitch (type I) fibre**, sometimes called white fibres, which are suited to short, rapid contractions such as sprinting or acceleration. Think of the breast muscle of a chicken – white, with very little fat and designed for short rapid and forceful contractions
- **fast twitch (type II) fibres**, sometimes called red fibres due to their rich blood supply. This type of fibre is suited to long-distance endurance riding. Think here of the leg muscle of chicken – darker meat due to the richer blood supply deep within the muscle.

Our leg muscles have a mixture of both fast twitch and slow twitch fibres, but the relative percentage is fixed by genetics and the only way they can be altered is by choosing different parents!

Sports training only affects the muscle fibres that are already there and makes them better at doing their job; it doesn't change the basic genetic type of the fibres. That said, of course, a rider's sprinting capabilities will be improved if they have the correct genetics, specific fitness training and technical expertise to realize that potential. Just because someone was born with an abundance of fast twitch fibres, they won't make a sprinter unless they practice. A top sprinter still has to complete the race distance and be there at the finish to contest the sprint, so endurance training cannot be overlooked. Likewise, a rider genetically predisposed to endurance work can improve their sprinting capabilities by targeted fitness and technique training, as well as by choosing to go for sprints over a longer distance than the last 50m (150ft) or so of the race as a pure sprinter might choose.

So how do you know which camp you are in? Without complex and invasive medical testing you will never really know, but looking in the mirror as well as appraising your strengths and weaknesses within your riding will provide useful clues. Once you have ascertained that you have a certain type of muscle characteristics and a genetic predisposition to particular type of activity, what happens when you start training?

Most cyclists, particularly road racers, fall into the ectomorph or mesomorph category.

As noted above, regular exercise improves the blood flow to the muscles. It also improves the rate at which oxygen is extracted by the muscle fibres into their cells and the rate at which that oxygen, together with the fuels supplied via the bloodstream, can be used to facilitate muscle contraction. The muscle fibres undergo structural changes, which mean they can contract not only quicker but also more forcefully. In cycling terms, this means the ability to pedal more quickly in a higher (harder) gear without fatigue. The improved blood supply in the trained muscle also means that waste products are transported away more effectively, so delaying the build-up of toxins and the associated muscle fatigue. One thing to note is that the total number of muscle fibres does not increase, only their size and volume. Coupled with the additional blood volume within a muscle, this makes the muscle appear bulkier and feel firmer.

Alongside these changes within the muscle cells there are also changes within the nerves that instruct the muscle fibres to contract. Think of the nerves as electrical wires that stimulate the muscle fibres to contract. With regular training, the number of these fine wires (nerve fibre endings) going deep into the muscle increases, so the electrical stimulation effect is stronger with more individual muscle fibres contracting at once. This means that for any given nerve impulse, the force of muscle contraction is stronger.

In an untrained muscle, many of the fibres are not directly connected to the electrical nerve impulses, so their contractile capacity is poor. With better blood supply and better transmission of nerve impulses, more muscle fibres can be stimulated to contract and the force and rate of this contraction can increase, that is, the maximal force the muscle can apply is increased.

During most riding, the muscles don't need to contract with maximum force, but if, say, riding at a certain speed requires 85 per cent effort within an untrained muscle, then due to the increased effectiveness of the systems within the trained muscle, it may mean that the same speed can be reached using only 65 per cent of capacity, thus leaving plenty of extra scope within the system – in short, the same outcome for less work.

These changes don't necessarily happen to all the muscle fibres simultaneously – it depends on the stress loads placed on them. This, in turn, will depend on the riding style and effort. For example, sprint training and real top-end extra-hard efforts will stimulate the sprinting fibres (type II – fast twitch) and so these will undergo physiological changes to help them to cope with this type of loading. Long, steady riding will overload the endurance fibres (type I – slow twitch) and promote changes in these. Hence, training needs to be both specific to the required end outcomes and also general in order to maintain a healthy balance within the systems. Furthermore, these changes will only take place in the actual muscles under load, be they the thigh, calf and buttock muscles during seated riding, or the trunk and upper body muscles during climbing efforts.

AEROBIC VERSUS ANAEROBIC

These are two words that crop up regularly within training manuals and relate to different types of activity within the muscle fibres. Aerobic literally means 'with air', in this case air being oxygen, and anaerobic means 'without air' (without oxygen). This relates to the way in which the muscle fibres make the energy required for muscle contraction.

To contract, muscle fibres need a special type of chemical fuel known as adenosine triphosphate (ATP). This is produced by breaking down nutrient fuels such as carbohydrates, proteins and fats, which are then supplied direct to the muscles in their component building blocks of simple sugars, amino acids and fatty acids, in molecules small enough to be carried via the bloodstream deep into the muscle cells.

Essentially, there are two ways that the cells can produce ATP from the sugars and amino acids. One method requires oxygen and the other does not. The aerobic, or oxygen-requiring process, produces nearly

Time trial riding is an aerobic activity demanding good blood supply to the working muscles.

ten times more ATP than the anaerobic method. In addition, the aerobic method produces water and carbon dioxide as waste products. Water is clearly harmless and the carbon dioxide is transported away by the blood back to the lungs and exhaled (inhaling more oxygen at the same time).

The anaerobic mechanism produces lactic acid as its waste product. A build-up of this chemical increases the acidity of the blood in the muscles (and ultimately the whole blood supply), resulting in feelings of cramp, pain and fatigue as the muscle fibres are essentially being poisoned. The good news is that, as soon as the levels of activity reduce and there is again sufficient oxygen available to meet the demand, this waste lactic acid can be metabolized safely to become carbon dioxide and water, allowing muscle activity to continue.

Provided that there is sufficient nutrient fuel available, aerobic activity within the muscles can theoretically continue indefinitely, whilst pure anaerobic activity can only last for a minute or so without a toxic build-up of acid. Think of aerobic activity as the mainstay and anaerobic activity as the 'top-up' mechanism for when a little extra 'oomph' is required, say, in a sprint or up a steep hill.

Finally, and perhaps most importantly, muscle activity is rarely 100 per cent aerobic or 100 per cent anaerobic. Most of the time there is a combination of both types of activity. Even at rest, it is estimated that 2 per cent of muscle energy is derived anaerobically – it is just that there is plenty of aerobic capacity within the muscles to use up the waste lactic acid and convert it to harmless end products. As the exercise level increases, so the percentage of anaerobic activity increases along with the rate of lactic acid production. At a certain level, the aerobic systems can't cope with getting rid of the lactic acid and it starts to build up, with painful consequences! This level of exertion

Riding hard uphill in a road race is an anaerobic activity.

is referred to as the 'lactate threshold' and one key end result of a good training plan is to increase the level of exertion that can be attained without reaching the lactate threshold – put simply, training can raise your lactate threshold so that you can race harder for longer.

Remember, too, that one of the effects of regular training is to improve the blood supply to the individual muscle cells. This increases the availability of oxygen and fuel to the muscle cells and thus helps to promote aerobic energy production. So a fit athlete will be able to work at a higher level aerobically than an unfit person and so is less likely to enter the anaerobic zone. Also, as it is the aerobic systems that get rid of excess lactic acid, a fit person will be able to recover more quickly from an anaerobic sprint burst.

Type I (slow twitch) muscle fibres are primarily involved in aerobic energy production, but are quickly poisoned by any build-up of lactic acid. Type II (fast twitch) fibres can work both aerobically or anaerobically, as required. They can also tolerate higher levels of lactic acid. This explains why a rider with a higher percentage of fast twitch fibres will be able to sprint better than one with a lower percentage and also why a rider with a higher percentage of type I fibres has better aerobic endurance capabilities.

In summary, each individual rider has a different muscle fibre make-up and training will serve to enhance the way in which those muscle fibres work and also help to compensate for potential shortfalls.

BASIC SPORTS NUTRITION

There many books available at all academic levels on nutrition for health and sports performance. Within the scope of this book we will only look at the direct requirements for cycle training and racing over and above a good, healthy diet.

Calorific Requirements

Cycling is often, and quite rightly, promoted as a great way of improving health and general fitness. It is a non-load bearing exercise, so unlike when running the joints don't take a pounding. Also, with modern gears cycling can be as hard or as easy as you want, making it an ideal exercise for even very unfit people. It is also relatively easy to sustain a cycling activity for an hour or more, whereas a gym session or fitness class would typically be shorter than that. At the opposite end of the spectrum, cycle racing is one of the toughest and most challenging sports in the world. What other sport entails competing for five to six hours per day for three weeks, like the Tour de France? In short, cycling is one of the most versatile and adaptable of sporting activities.

The calorific requirement of any activity is directly related to the level of intensity coupled with the duration of effort. When looking at the calorific burn of any activity we must focus on the additional calories used over and above what would have been consumed if we'd stayed at home watching the television or sitting at the office desk. The average female burns around 2,000 calories (8,000kilojoules) per day and the average male some 2,400 calories (10,000kJ), which, broadly speaking, translates into 150–200 (600–800kJ) calories per hour whilst awake.

Running at a moderately hard pace might burn off an additional 400–500 calories (1,600–2,000kJ) per hour, with most running sessions lasting around an hour (or less). Cycling at a similar effort, because you are seated and weight-supported, might only use 300 or so extra calories per hour, but you are likely to be able to continue at that pace for two hours or more.

On the converse, because of the gears and fact you can freewheel downhill it is easy to cycle at a much lower effort or intensity than

you can run at, so a three-hour really slow bike ride might indeed burn fewer calories than a forty-five-minute hard, fast run. To increase your calorie burn, the rides need to be moderately hard and around ninety minutes to two hours in duration. Fortunately, this type of riding is ideal for improvements in cycle race fitness as well as for health and weight control.

Fat Burning

One of the biggest misconceptions in cycling and weight management is the concept of long, slow riding being good for 'fat burning'. If this were true, then the elite racing cyclists would all be on the podgy side and the mile-eating cyclotourists all mega-skinny. There is quite obviously something flawed in this argument! Certainly, the fuel for long, steady miles will come largely from the metabolism of fat. However, the rate of calorie burn is quite slow and it is easy actually to consume calories, in the form of snacks and energy bars, at a faster rate than you are using them on this type of ride.

Faster riding at a manageable but moderate work rate will increase the total number of calories burnt. Although a lower percentage of calories consumed may come from fat, the fact that the total number is greater means that you actually end up burning more fat calories by riding at this brisker pace.

Short, hard racing or training efforts are fuelled almost entirely from carbohydrate and protein derived calories. However, this sort of riding has a high calorific burn rate and increases your metabolic rate. This, in turn, means that, by the end of the day, you'll have used up a significant total number of calories, of which a good percentage will have come from fat metabolism whilst recovering from the training.

The table opposite summarises these three different types of riding and how they fit into a race training and weight-control plan.

The Three Different Types of Riding		
Ride Type	Training Benefit	Weight-Control Benefit
Long, steady riding – two or more hours at a pace at which you can easily hold a conversation	Miles in the saddle strengthen the support- ing muscles, improve all-round blood flow and improve stamina	Fairly low calorie burn per hour, but makes up for it in the total number of hours of riding that can be achieved – just be careful you don't put all the calories back in at the café stop
Moderate intensity –typically sixty–ninety minutes of riding time	Maximum training ben- efits in terms of aerobic fitness and endurance – the ability to work at a good effort rate for a sustained period	Fairly high calorie burn, including fat calories; best training mode for weight loss as can be sustained for reasonable time period
Fast, short, intense and hard riding	Race-specific speed and strength, improves top- end power and climb- ing abilities	High calorific burn, plus changes to muscles increase resting metabolic rate and so day-to-day calorie burn; in short, the reason elite cyclists are so lean

Fuelling Your Training

In order to fuel your training, you must ensure that you are putting the right type of fuel into the body and at the right time. Just like a car, the body must have fuel in the system for it to perform. Training without the necessary fuel is, at best, going to have limited benefit and at worst could cause serious problems.

The best approach is to ensure that there is sufficient fuel in the system before you set off on your training ride or race. Different people seem to be able to train hard after very differing time frames post-eating. This will also depend on what you have eaten. Typically, easier-to-digest foods can be eaten closer to the training time and the easier the training session, the closer to it you can eat.

For a race event or high-intensity session, you might only be able to tolerate having eaten two hours before riding, but for a steady miles session a light snack before you leave might be okay.

Putting the fuel in before you ride not only fuels the training effort, but also in terms of weight control you put the additional calo- ries in and burn them off, leaving few excess calories in the system.

Early morning training or race events are the hardest to cater for. Practise your chosen regime in training so that you know what works best for you before your first race. A bowl of cereal with a whey protein-based supplement, or a low-fat cheese spread sand- wich, or a bowl of low-fat rice pudding along with plenty of water or dilute energy drink taken about sixty–ninety minutes before the session (maybe two hours before for a hard race) works well for most people. Although brown bread and wholegrain cereals may be

Using two bottle cages helps you carry enough energy drink for long training rides.

better for overall nutrition, for a pre-training meal you want something easy and quick to digest, so opt for white bread, white rice and the like and save your whole grains for non-training days.

Do try to ensure that you include protein in your pre-training meal, as it is important for fuelling performance as well as in the post-training recovery and muscle adaptation. Try to keep the fat content down as it will slow the digestion process.

Training in the evening after work can also present problems. One sensible option is to have a double-lunch. Eating your lunch a little earlier than usual and then having a mid-afternoon snack will mean you aren't training on an empty stomach and won't need such a big meal after training. Furthermore, by moving some of the evening calories to earlier in the day you are putting the calories into the training rather than onto your waistline.

Suitable foods for a mid-afternoon snack might be a tuna and pasta salad, a rice salad, a lean meat sandwich or a jacket potato. You might also consider using a proprietary energy drink with your snack to ensure a good mix of carbohydrates along with the protein and fat of the snack. Cereal bars or special energy bars work well too, but do check the fat content isn't too high (more than about 7–8 per cent). The fat in a snack bar suitable for training and racing should contribute less than 30 per cent of the calories.

After training you will need to refuel and rehydrate. How much you need to take on board in terms of calories will depend on whether or not you are trying to loose some excess weight and when your next training ride or race is.

Many of the sports science training manuals refer to a 'magic window' that occurs some twenty–sixty minutes after exercise when the systems of the body are at their optimum for refuelling. Whilst it is very important to ensure that you replenish spent energy supplies as soon as possible after exercise, if you are in a stage race or on a training camp where you are riding day after day at a hard level, for the majority of riders a more gradual approach to refuelling may be better. After all, if, for example, you have done a two-hour endurance ride on a Sunday morning, with Monday typically being a rest day, the next time you train might well be Tuesday evening. Under those circumstances, a normal, well-balanced diet will suffice to ensure that the energy stores are replenished without risking consuming surplus calories.

If, however, you are due to train or race the next day, you must replace the spent calories and top up your energy reserves. The best way to do this is by having a simple carbohydrate, energy rich snack or drink as soon as possible after your ride. Recovery drinks and bars are ideal, but any wholesome low-fat cereal bar will be almost as good. You also need to ensure that you rehydrate fully, so take on board plenty of water or dilute energy drink.

If you are trying to lose some weight and aren't due for a hard session the next day, then a light protein-rich snack should be sufficient. If, however, you find yourself light-headed, take in some extra calories. Furthermore, a heavy meal late in the evening just prior to bed is a sure way of putting on the pounds – hence the idea of taking in the additional calories earlier in the day before the training and then just a light supper before bed.

Sports Drinks and Hydration

Having the correct fuel in the body is important, but even more crucial is ensuring that you keep yourself hydrated. This applies not only during training and racing, but also before and after riding – for example, just a 1 per cent reduction in hydration levels can result in a 10 per cent reduction in performance; a loss of 25 per cent or more fluid will have serious medical consequences.

For shorter rides plain water will be fine – around 500ml per hour in cool weather and up to a litre on very hot days. However, by virtue of complex molecular science, water is absorbed more quickly into the body if the drink contains a small amount of salts and sugars. Such drinks are referred to as hypotonic, electrolyte or rehydration formulations and are ideal for short summer rides or if you are prone to sweating. Remember though – the salts and sugars in these drinks are at a very low level and are there to promote hydration. They are not there in a high enough amount to provide energy. You can cheaply and easily make your own hypotonic hydration drink by mixing 20ml of fresh orange juice into a 750ml bottle of water and adding a very small pinch of table salt.

For energy replacement, you need what is referred to as an isotonic drink, as opposed to an electrolyte one that is just for mineral salt replacement. Some formulas will do both, but read the labels to make sure. Energy drink formulas contain what are known as complex or long-chain carbohydrates which break down at a steady rate, releasing energy into the bloodstream in a controlled manner – they don't simply provide a burst of sugar, but provide a more sustained energy supply. The electrolyte formulas aid hydration with the added bonus of replacing salts lost through sweat, thereby reducing the risks of cramps and muscle spasms.

As these isotonic drinks provide a steady supply of fuel rather than a single shot, you should start using them early into a ride. If your ride is going to be more than sixty minutes long or you weren't able to eat much in the hours leading up it, these drinks will be a big bonus. Aim to drink one 500ml bottle per hour – topping up to 750ml per hour by adding extra water if it's hot or you are prone to sweating. This will aid both energy supply and prevent hydration.

The further you are into a ride, the more important the hydration element is, as you should have been keeping your energy stores topped up so far. For this reason, on a typical two-hour summer endurance training ride one bottle of energy formula and one bottle of hydration/electrolyte formula will be ideal. In the winter, two energy formula bottles might be more appropriate.

For a short, hard training ride or a race of less than one hour, assuming you topped up the energy stores previously, one bottle of energy drink will be fine. Then, on returning home, drink a bottle of the rehydration/electrolyte formula – or your homemade mix – to aid muscle recovery. Some proprietary recovery formula drinks also contain protein, which can aid recovery, especially after long or hard training sessions.

For long, steady rides alternate energy and hydration, remembering that energy is more important in the first half of the ride and hydration in the second.

So, in summary, you need to ensure that you are well hydrated and your energy tanks are full prior to training and racing. You need to balance your calorific intake with the duration and intensity of your riding. Whilst ensuring sufficient energy is available during training, keeping well hydrated is more important. A good healthy and balanced diet with plenty of carbohydrate and lean protein, along with a healthy level of fat intake, will ensure that your body can refuel between exercise sessions.

SCIENTIFIC APPROACHES TO TRAINING

In the past, cycle training simply involved riding a bike and the more miles you did, so much the better. The only training diary a racing cyclist had was a weekly mileage chart. Sunday club rides of six hours or more were commonplace, with 100-mile (160km) rides the staple of winter training.

Interval training – bouts of higher intensity effort interspersed with recovery – was introducing into cycle training in the 1980s, to a mixed reception. However, as people's lifestyles changed and individuals couldn't afford the time to train for fifteen or more hour per week, so the concept of prescribed

Training Zone Levels		
Normal conversation	Zone 1	Easy riding
Short paragraphs	Zone 2	Light to moderate work rate
Sentences	Zone 3	Moderate work rate but manageable
Phrases	Zone 4	Hard work but just about okay
Odd words	Zone 5	Very hard work, just manageable
Grunts	Zone 6	Maximal effort

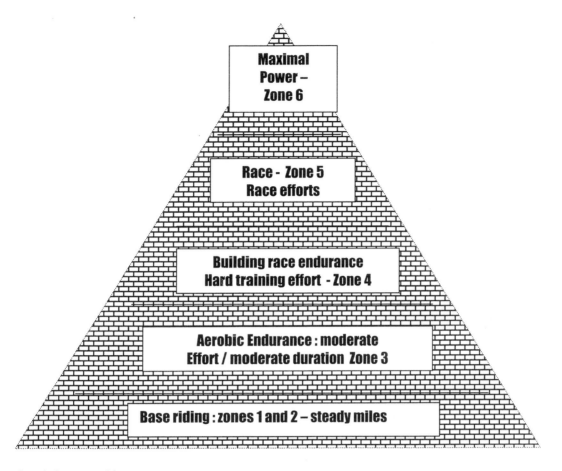

A training pyramid.

and dedicated training sessions gained in popularity. Today, with our greater understanding of sports science and the physiological processes involved in training, training methods have advanced even further. Professional coaches can prescribe training not just in terms of miles and hours, but right down to the specific power output (wattage) and heart rate that a rider must sustain.

Fortunately, many of these scientific principles can be simplified and applied even to the novice rider, allowing for each training ride to enhance a specific element of your riding. One of the most important tools within your training is known as Perceived Effort, or PE. By gauging how hard you are

trying and for how long you are holding that effort, you can gauge different training sessions. One very basic but scientifically valid test of PE is the 'talk test'. Imagine a group of cyclists riding along together and chatting away. As soon as the terrain becomes hilly and the riders start to climb, the breathing rates go up and the level of conversation comes down. The riders crest the hill and as they recover, so the conversation level increases again. We can use this concept to divide training effort into a number of different levels or zones (*see* table below).

Most training plans will involve a certain amount of training in each of the different zones – starting by building a sound endurance and stamina base by plenty of riding at zones 1 and 2. After this period of base-building work, some shorter but harder sessions at zones 3 and 4 might be introduced, but keeping some rides at zone 1 and 2 to ensure the stamina base doesn't suffer.

As most races, depending on the distance of the course, take place in the zone 4 region, with some work at zone 5, the training plan will need to introduce sessions at race intensity. Furthermore, as very few races are completely flat, some top-end work at zone 6 might be included, but only once the rider had completed plenty of zone 4/5 type training.

The end result of such a periodized training programme is to create a pyramid effect, with a broad base of training at zone 1 supporting the layers of zone 2 and above, culminating in a small peak at zone 6.

By visualizing the training plan as a brick-built pyramid, each ride you do adds bricks to the pyramid in the corresponding intensity layer. So a two-hour steady and easy paced ride will add in bricks at the base at zone 1. A two-hour ride over rolling terrain where you had to work harder on the hills might add in, say, an hour's worth of training bricks at zone 1, forty minutes at zone 2 and twenty minutes at zone 3 or even 4.

The main thing is to keep the balance of training appropriate to your race aims – and remember to start your training at the base levels before adding in the harder intensity work. That said, there is little point doing hours and hours of slow, steady base riding and nothing else. Whilst this may make you feel like a cyclist, your race performance and speed will be sadly lacking. On the other hand, someone who constantly rides for twenty or thirty minutes flat out is more likely ultimately to suffer from overtraining or chronic fatigue, as their base training won't be sufficient to support their race training.

PERIODIZED OR BLOCK TRAINING

The most effective way to structure your training is to build gradually through the layers of the training pyramid, allocating specific aims to each training block. By allowing recovery both within and between the blocks, you should be able to increase your fitness levels with minimal risk of overtraining.

Such a balanced approach might look something like the plan shown here, although the length of each training block will depend on the individual. It is better to spend a week or so longer within each block than progress too quickly. Similarly, you should include an easier week every now and again within the plan – maybe every fourth or sixth week. This will help you to recover more quickly from the training load and allow your body to adapt better to the training load.

Phase 1: Base Fitness

Phase 1 consists of seven weeks of training and starts fifteen weeks before the race day. This initial training block is about getting used to riding the bike while building endurance and stamina. Your ultimate aim is to compete in a race of around thirty–sixty minutes, so building up to riding for two hours at a moderate pace is the training plan. Keep your riding at a comfortable pace at zone 1 or 2. Some of these rides should be in groups, especially if a bunch road race is your aim. Vary the terrain so that you get used to long drags as well as hills and cornering becomes second nature.

Ride three to five times per week for at least one hour, gradually increasing the average speed of your rides as well as the duration. Try to do one two-hour ride each week. You should also include one recovery ride, consisting of thirty minutes of very light, easy riding, in which you focus on smooth pedalling rather than speed.

Phase 1 consists of six solid weeks' riding, during which time you should come to feel a lot more comfortable on the bike, as well as fitter and quicker. The seventh week should be a rest week with just two short and easy rides. This will allow the body to recuperate and adapt to the training load before progressing onto the next layer of training.

Phase 2: Adding in Race-Pace Endurance

Phase 2 consists of five weeks of training and starts eight weeks before the race day. With a good base fitness in place after Phase 1, you can now start to build towards race-specific training, culminating, perhaps, your first training race session.

Continue riding three to five rides per week, with one of these still being a two-hour endurance ride. For the other sessions, include two out of the following speed sessions per week, plus at least one easy recovery ride:

- sixty minutes of riding at a fast pace (zones 3–4) for the middle thirty–forty minutes
- eighty minutes of mixed-pace riding – riding at a moderate effort (zone 2), but adding in some extra effort on the hills and on some faster stretches of road. Try to include a total of thirty minutes of hard-level work (zone 3 and 4)
- forty-five minutes of speed work – after a ten-minute warm-up ride for five minutes going as fast as possible, ease off for five minutes of recovery riding. Repeat the five-minute effort plus five-minute recovery a total of four times (over forty minutes), then cool down. Practise racing, so ride on the drop handlebars if possible; or, if practising for time trials and you have fitted clip-on time trial bars, practise riding on these.

Remember to keep your recovery session or sessions going. These should, as in the first block, be a short light ride, no longer than forty minutes at zone 1, focusing on relaxing on the bike and doing light, fast pedalling. With the increasingly harder sessions, you might need to do two recovery sessions this week, alongside two of the speed sessions and the endurance session.

Four weeks of speed work will pay dividends and you can reward yourself with another easy recovery week to let the training bed in.

Phase 3: Race Speed and Taper

Phase 3 consists of three weeks of training and starts three weeks before the race day. This racing preparation plan finishes with three weeks of race-specific preparation and tapering. (A taper is a period of reduced-intensity or easier training or riding and rest prior to an event, to ensure the rider is well rested prior to a race.)The format of this will depend upon the type of race you are preparing for and is covered in the next chapter, but basically the time trial rider will now focus on preparing for a thirty-minute hard but sustained effort, whereas the road race rider will be aiming for fifty–sixty minutes of mixed fast/slow riding.

POST-RACE TRAINING

After successfully completing your first race you will hopefully want to go on and do more events or try out a different race type. After the race, you need to give your body a week to recover and then maybe pick the training plan up again from Phase 2, this time with just two weeks of race endurance training and then two weeks from Phase 3 as speed training.

After these four weeks of training, another taper week can take you to your second key race. In the meantime, training races and club time trials can still form part of your race training, but, at least in the first instance, try not to target more than one race per month. This should allow you to improve your base fitness as well as race-specific training.

Ideally, you should include some Phase 1 type training not just at the start of your race career, but every month or so after that, with a longer period of base training during the winter. Balancing the different types of training in the ratio of seven–five–three will help to keep your 'pyramid' strong and secure – remember the analogy that you need a strong foundation to build a tall structure and the peak can only be as high as the base will support. You might also decide to enlist a coach to help you plan your training and racing and focus on specific goals and targets.

CHAPTER 5

Planning and Event Selection

There is a great variety of competitive cycling events on the road, ranging from easy events such as circuit races that take place on a closed road circuit, through to stage races covering vast distances and requiring a great deal of support and equipment. Cycle racing on the road does not have to be complicated and the events that you can take part in competitively are not difficult to find once you know where to look. The vast majority of races are run by cycling clubs and not, as is the case in some sports, large commercial enterprises. This has advantages to the competitive cyclist, such as lower entry fees and the knowledge that the organizers are involved in the sport and are putting something back into cycling. The downside of the cycle club organizers is that they probably work during the day and may not be available to answer your queries or questions relating to the race when you would like to get in touch with them, although most race organizers will be helpful and keen to have you in their event. The two main governing bodies of British cycling, British Cycling and the Cycle Time Trials (CTT), are the main sources of cycle races in the UK. (For further details of all organizations cited in this chapter, *see* Appendix.)

So, now you've got the bike, got the kit, done the training and are all geared up for your first event. This chapter and the following one are designed to help prepare you for your first proper event – be that a solo time trial or a bunch road race. We will look at choosing your first event, your training over the last couple of weeks prior to the event, getting you and your bike ready and the event itself. The aim is to ensure you are prepared mentally as well as physically for the challenge in order that the race goes as smoothly and enjoyably as possible, leaving you keen for more.

SELECTING YOUR FIRST EVENT

Hopefully by now you will have decided whether you want to start your racing career with a group road race or a solo ride in a time trial. If not, then now is the time to decide! If you've done most of your training riding in groups and relish the idea of directly racing with others, the road race option would be the obvious choice. However, if you are bit unsure of your group riding skills and have done most of your riding alone, maybe a solo time trial would be a better starting point.

Choosing and Entering Your First Road Race

The majority of official road race events are run under the banner of British Cycling. To ride in these events, you normally need to be a member of this organization, although for some events you can take out a one-day membership, but you will need to find this out in advance. In terms of choosing your first race event proper, it is best to look for a race designed for novice racers. There are several of these and they are usually held on closed traffic-free circuits. They are usually around forty-five minutes to an hour in duration, lapping around a circuit typically of 1–3 miles (1.6–4.8km).

The best way to find a suitable event is to do an Internet search. British Cycling's novice races are currently under the

ENTRY FORM FOR ROAD & CIRCUIT RACES UNDER THE TECHNICAL REGULATIONS OF BRITISH CYCLING

To the Organiser: (PLEASE USE BLOCK CAPITALS)

Event name:		Date of race:		Category of race:	*see the handbook or*
Title: (Mr/Miss/Mrs)		Date of birth:		I enclose entry fee of:	£
First Name:		Surname:			
Address:					
Town:		County:			
Postcode:		Home Telephone:			
My E-mail address:		Date entered:			
BC Licence No:	*this is on your licence or write – not applicable or licence applied for*	UCI code:	*again on the licence*		
Category:	*you will start off as a 4ᵗʰ Cat rider*	Club/Team:			
Registered Colours:	*the colours of your club kit or plain if private member*	I am not prepared to be nominated as a reserve:	☐ *tick this box if you want to be a reserve in the event of the race being full*		
Key sponsors:	*of your club !*				

Licence points gained: (if applicable)		Premier calendar points gained: (if applicable)	
Last season:	This season	Last season:	This season:

Best performances in British Cycling or UCI sanctioned events this year and last year: : if nil write NIL on the first line

	Placing	Name of Event:	Date:	Distance:	Category:	Name of Winner:
1						
2						
3						
4						

DECLARATION-
I declare that I am eligible under British Cycling Technical Regulations to enter this race and that the information on this form is complete and correct. I understand and agree that I participate in this race entirely at my own risk, that I must rely on my own ability in dealing with all hazards and that I must ride in a manner which is safe for myself and all others. I am aware that when riding in an event and particularly when riding on a public highway the function of the marshals is only to indicate direction and that I must decide if the movement is safe. I agree that no liability whatsoever shall be attached to the promoter, promoting club, meeting sponsor(s), British Cycling, or any official or member of the British Cycling or member of the promoting club in respect of any injury, loss or damage suffered by me in or by reason of the race, however caused.

Signed	*(and don't forget to sign your entry)*

ENTRIES WITHOUT CORRECT FEE OR DETAILS WILL NOT BE ACCEPTED

Entry forms are available from Membership & Event Services, British Cycling, National Cycling Centre, Stuart Street, Manchester M11 4DQ Tel: 0870 871 2000. Fax 0870 871 2001 Copyright BCF 2004

A road race entry form.

'Go-Race' banner. Their lowest category of standard races is category C or Regional C+, but do bear in mind that some of the riders in these events will be much more experienced than you.

Within British Cycling, riders are classified as well as events. Full details can be found on its website, but essentially novice riders start off as fourth category riders. You collect points by being placed in events (see below) and as you collect points you move up the category system through third, second and first category to elite, which includes professional and semi-professional riders as well as the top amateurs. Junior riders (under eighteens) are categorized fourth to first on a similar basis. To move up from fourth to third category, you 'only' need ten points, so fourth category events are specifically aimed at the novice or weaker rides.

The different event categories relate to the number of points available within that race, which reflect the distance and duration of the event and also which class of riders it is open to. A lower-category event will have fewer points available and so won't attract the point-hunting, more experienced riders. On this basis, it makes sense to choose a fourth category rider-only race in the points category 5 (Regional C+ or Regional B) or a Regional C event which doesn't qualify for any licence points. ('Regional' events are intended to be more local events, as oppose to national events. You should come across more local riders and therefore could assume the racing may be a little easier.)

The over-forties can also ride special veterans' road race events in conjunction with both British Cycling and the League of Veteran Racing Cyclists (LVRC). Whilst these are normally very friendly events and the standard of bike handling is good, the categorization is based on age, not ability, and there are some very fast and fit riders.

Getting started in racing may sound rather complicated, but in reality it is very straightforward. Speaking with fellow riders, club mates and being friendly with your local cycle shop owners is the best way to learn the system. They will also know your ability and can perhaps best advise you on which events are the most suitable.

Your first event is more than likely on one of the closed race circuits, so it makes sense to get some practise riding on these types of roads. Often there are training sessions held at the circuit race venues and these will provide an excellent way of getting familiar with the course and of riding in groups on what can be quite twisting and narrow roads. Often these training sessions incorporate handicap training races or you might find that the local club organizes such an event on another evening. In a handicap event the slower riders are set off in a small group first, followed after a time interval by the next group of slightly more experienced and faster riders and so on, with the 'scratch' group setting off last and consisting of the faster riders. Each group has to catch the ones in front, with the winner being the rider who crosses the finishing line first. This format gives the novice rider the opportunity to practise racing on a race circuit at speed but within, initially, a smaller group. The group will swell in size as the faster riders catch up, but as the novice group improves so the likelihood of not getting caught increases and the first 'win' beckons.

In addition to training sessions at the race venue, handicap or other training races you should aim to get as much practise as possible riding in groups at speed. This will help your bike-handling skills, your reaction times and your confidence, so when you finally get to the start line in your first event proper things won't seem so daunting.

So let's assume you've identified the event you want to target. You need then to join the appropriate organization as required and send off your entry form well in advance. Keep a copy of the event details together with your racing licence (if required), as many events do not send any information out directly to the competitors. The further in

OPPOSITE: *British Cycling is the main body that governs both professional and amateur group road racing in the UK.*

advance you identify your first event, the better you can structure your training and preparation. Be aware that many events have entry deadlines, so make sure you get the entry in early. Apart from anything else, this means that if you make a mistake in the entry you'll have time to make amends before the deadline. Phone the organizer if you have any queries, but do remember that most of them are volunteers. A few events have their own website, linked via the British Cycling events calendar webpage, and some have on-line entry, which is likely to increase in popularity in the future.

As already noted, British Cycling is the governing body for most types of cycle competition, from mountain bike and Cyclo-Cross events to road races and time trials. The majority of time trials in the UK are run through the CTT, although some are still with British Cycling and in Scotland the majority are with British Cycling. This does make things a little more complicated, but essentially between these two organizations you will find the type of event you are looking for.

Initially, we will look at the British Cycling system for competition in road (or circuit) events. There are three ways to find British Cycling events, firstly the annual *British Cycling Handbook*. This publication comes out in the first two months of the year and is supported by the regular monthly magazine of British Cycling, *Racing Calendar*, which will highlight any new events or any cancelled or amended events. The format lists the date of the event and the region in which it takes place. This will help you to narrow down the general area of the event; a map at the front of the book will clarify the geographical location of the region in question. The title of the event is next and the type of event will then be listed. Road races will be listed as such and circuit races will also be of interest, especially for the novice. The event details will include the location and start time. The location will generally stipulate the race headquarters, but this may not give you a clear idea about where you will be racing. This is where contact with the organizer will be required to establish the nature of the course. The race organizer's details are

there for this purpose and to allow you to send in the appropriate entry form. The race details section will also highlight the categories that the race is open to, as well as the exact start time and the distance of the race. Racing under British Cycling rules is split into categories. This starts at fourth category for novices through to first category for experienced successful competitors and elite for the very best in the country. Moving through the categories is achieved through success in events. Races of different distances offer different points, depending on the position you finish and the race classification or band. For example seventh place in a band 3 event will give you 10 points – the same as winning a band 5 race. The more points on offer, the more likely the racing is to be hotly contested. If you are simply looking as a novice to complete your first road race, then a band 5 event with few points on offer is better place to start than a higher-banded race. Furthermore, the lower band events are typically shorter in distance:

Band	1	2	3	4	5
Position	Nat A Road / Nat A Circuit	Nat B Road / Nat B Circuit	Reg A Road / Reg A Circuit	Reg B Road / Reg B Circuit	Reg C+
1	100	60	30	15	10
2	85	52	25	12	8
3	75	45	21	10	7
4	66	40	17	8	6
5	58	35	14	6	5
6	51	31	12	5	4
7	45	27	10	4	3
8	39	23	8	3	2
9	34	20	7	2	1
10	29	17	6	1	1
11	25	15	5		
12	21	13	4		
13	18	11	3		
14	15	9	2		
15	12	7	1		
16	10	6			
17	8	5			
18	6	3			

Young and old can mix together happily in the bunch.

By finishing in a points-winning position you will score points on your licence (providing you don't have a day licence). Once you have scored six points you will move from a fourth-category rider to a third-category rider. You then need to score a further thirty points to move from third to second category. Once you are a second-category rider you need to score twenty points in a year to keep this category and if you score one hundred points you will become a first-category rider. The majority of people racing in road races in the UK are third-category riders. This category has a wide variety of riders within it, but you should be able to find races for fourth-category riders that are accessible and will suit your abilities. The licence mentioned above is available from British Cycling and you must have a racing licence to take part in British Cycling events. The licence comes with membership of the British Cycling Federation and this membership will also ensure that you receive the handbook.

If you want to try racing without taking out a full membership you can join for the day, which will allow you to try racing without the financial commitment of full membership. Race organizers will be able to sell you day membership and a day licence. However, any points that you may win will not be registered with British Cycling.

To enter the race, you will need to submit an official race entry form. The best place to find these is on the relevant website, where you can download them. The form is quite self-explanatory for the novice as there are several boxes that cannot be completed. Simply complete your name and address along with your cycling club (if you have one) and the race you want to enter. If you have a licence you need to add the number and category. If you are not a member of a club you need to ride in kit that is plain. This means no replica team kits or kit with the name of sponsors on it. Events need to be entered well in advance and at least two weeks before race day. A phrase you may hear is 'enter on the line', or EOL. This, as the name suggests, is the ability to enter the event on the day of the race. There is often

an increased price for this and the risk that the event could be full, but if you arrive nice and early you will probably get in, although, as always, a brief discussion with the organizer will help to clarify things.

Now you have selected and entered a race, next you need to ensure that you are clear about the rules. The *British Cycling Rulebook* is a heavy bit of reading, but worthwhile to ensure that you don't come into adverse contact with the race commissaires (race referees). These officials will be able to provide some guidance on the day, plus will give a race briefing twenty to thirty minutes before the race starts. This will detail the local rules as well as outlining any of the commissaires' particular favourite rules! The majority of rules are about ensuring safe racing for all, from basic rules such as helmets (hard-shell, cycling-specific) being compulsory, to not crossing the centre of the road if racing on the open road. Your race may have a neutralized section at the beginning, which means no racing for the first lap. This type of information will help you to understand what will happen in the first few minutes of the race.

To ensure that you get all the information you need and to guarantee a place in your race of choice if booking on the day, aim to arrive early (more than one hour before), so that you can drive or ride around the course, get changed in plenty of time and ensure your bike is well set up.

Choosing and Entering Your First Time Trial Event

In England and Wales time trials are run under the umbrella of Cycling Time Trials (CTT). In Scotland they fall under British Cycling. To ride a time trial you normally need to be a member of a club that is affiliated to the CTT, or in Scotland a member of British Cycling. The CTT website lists all the clubs grouped according to their district. Each district is allocated a code which goes back to the days when cycle racing on the highways was a highly secretive pastime and even today decoding the system isn't that straightforward. One of the benefits of

CYCLING TIME TRIALS

Est. 2002
the national governing body for CYCLING time trials
www.ctt.org.uk
1937 - 2002

RTTC

UNDER CYCLING TIME TRIALS REGULATIONS.
(National Championships are also under CHAMPIONSHIP CONDITIONS)
See Handbook for notifications of improvements. The Promoting Club reserves the right to refuse any entry (Subject to BBAR Condition No. 4)

Please enter me for the

_____

event to be held for and on behalf of Cycling Time Trials on (date)

I enclose entry fee of £ _____ Including Cycling Time Trials Levy.

If entering a Hill Climb please also complete section B. overleaf.
If entering a Team Time Trial please also complete section C. overleaf.

RIDING: Bicycle☐ Tricycle☐ Tandem☐

For Tandem Events my partner is:-

_____

If the event is oversubscribed I agree to be a reserve.
Yes☐ No☐

Mr/Mrs/Miss/Ms	Forename(s):-		Surname:-	
Club:-				District:-
Address:-				
			Postcode :-	
Tel:-	Mob:-	D.O.B.:-	Age on day of event:-	
E-mail:-			Start/Result Sheet by E-mail ☐	
Emergency Contact Details		Name:-		
Address:-				
Tel:-		Mob:-		

For Veterans Only

| Best Plus for distance in current and past three seasons. | | Age at that time | | Yrs. |
| Current Standard time for event entered. | | Member of VTTA Group | | |

OFFICIAL TIME TRIALS (including private) CLUB, OPEN, SEMI-OPEN AND ASSOCIATION EVENTS (completed events only.)
(For NATIONAL CHAMPIONSHIPS only enter performances in Open, Semi-Open and Association events.)
Please enter details of fastest performances during current and past three seasons for the type of machine you will be riding.
If no performance please state NIL.

Official use only Handicap:-

A.			Event	Date	Time/Distance	Course	Winner & Time/Distance
	10	1	you will need to record these details				
	25	2	for each of the events you ride for				
	50	3	future reference - for your first				
	100	4	event simply write nil in each column				
	12hr	5	However if you've ridden a club 10 then				
Fastest performance at		6	add the information to lines 1, 6 and 7				
Fastest performance ever		7					

I HEREBY DECLARE that the particulars submitted on this form are complete and correct. I understand that the event will be held under the Rules and Regulations of Cycling Time Trials as shown in the current Handbook and I confirm that I am conversant with such Rules and Regulations and undertake to abide by them and to participate in the Drug Testing Programme whenever required to do so.
I further declare that I am at present not under suspension by Cycling Time Trials or any organisation with which Cycling Time Trials have an agreement or (if so) such suspension will have expired by the date of the event.
I agree to accept the decision of the promoter in all the matters concerning the event and my participation in it subject to such rights of appeal or review as may be provided for in the Rules and Regulations of Cycling Time Trials.
I understand that the event is held wholly or in part on public or private property or the public highway and that I participate therein entirely at my own risk and that no liability whatever shall attach to the promoter, promoting club or any officials of the event, Cycling Time Trials or any member of such club for any injury loss or damage suffered by me in or by reason of the event however such may be caused and whether by negligence or otherwise.

Signature_____ Date _____
(Event promoters MUST NOT accept entries with photocopied signatures)
Riders under 18 years of age must also have the Parental Consent Declaration (overleaf) completed by their Parent or Guardian.
Cycling Time Trials is a Company Limited by Guarantee (Registered England No. 4413282)

January 2007

Cycling time trials entry form 1.

B.	**Hill Climb entrants please complete this section**						

Forename(s):- _____ Surname:- _____ Club:- _____

Best 3 performances in Cycling Time Trials approved Hill Climbs since 1st Jan. of previous 2 years. _For NATIONAL CHAMPIONSHIPS only enter performances in Open, Semi-Open and Association events_

DATE	NAME OF EVENT	NAME OF HILL	CLASS OF EVENT (Open, Semi-Open, Club,)	WINNER & TIME	MY PLACING	No. of Entries	MY TIME
DETAILS OF LAST 2 HILL CLIMBS							

C.	**Team Time Trial Details**

Please enter the details of **ALL** the team members and any reserves below

Rider 1 Name & Club		Rider 3 Name & Club		1st Reserve Name & Club	
Rider 2 Name & Club		Rider 4 Name & Club		2nd Reserve Name & Club	

PARENTAL CONSENT

TO BE SIGNED BY PARENT OR GUARDIAN OF ENTRANTS UNDER THE AGE OF 18

I (Name and Address) _____ Being the Parent (or Guardian) of _____ Who was born on: _____

HEREBY AGREE to his/her participation in the events promoted for and on behalf of Cycling Time Trials under their Rules and Regulations and DECLARE as follows:-

1 I understand and agree that my said son/daughter participates in events promoted under the Companys Rules and Regulations, entirely at his/her risk and without liability whatever on the part of CYCLING TIME TRIALS, its Chairman, National Committee Members, District Committee Members, Officers and Officials of member clubs, Event Secretaries (promoters), Timekeepers, Marshals, Course Measurers, Caterers or helpers in the conduct of the event in respect of any injury loss or damage suffered by him/her however caused whether by negligence or otherwise.
2 I understand that the function of the marshals in such events is to do no more than indicate the precise spot at which the rider should turn or the direction he or she should take and that the responsibility for safely negotiating a turn or any other change of direction must rest with the rider alone.
3 I understand further that all competitors in or in the vicinity of the event must observe the law of the land relating to road travel and when racing must ride entirely alone and unassisted.
4 I am satisfied that my son/daughter is sufficiently responsible and experienced to assume full and entire responsibility for his/her own safety whilst engaged in a competition of this kind held wholly or in part on public or private property or on the public highway.

Signature_____ Date_____
(Event promoters MUST NOT accept entries with photocopied signatures)

Cycling time trials entry form 2.

A TT gets under way.

ABOVE: *Knowing where the start is will be an obvious help!* BELOW: *The rider in an upright position through a left handed curve during a time trial.*

joining a local club is that there will be people there who can help you to decipher the code!

There are basically two different types of time trials – club events, usually run on rural courses on summer weekday evenings, and Open events, which usually run at weekends. Open events are what are classified as 'proper' time trials with a formal entry process, results sheet and the like, whereas club events are more informal and you can just turn up and ride, provided you are a member of an affiliated club. One exception to that are the 'come-and-try-it' events that some clubs run during the summer. Some clubs will let you ride your first event under this banner, joining afterwards if you wish to continue.

Joining a club is usually a simple matter of completing a form and handing over the membership fee. However, sometimes membership has to be approved by the club committee, which will meet only monthly or bimonthly, so you need to plan ahead in order that your membership is active when you enter your first Open event.

Club evening time trials are normally held over the 10-mile (16km) distance, although sometimes there are longer events when daylight permits, or non-standard distance events such as a 7.8-mile (12.5km) hilly loop. The 10-mile race is a good distance to start with. Whilst the top riders might complete this at near 30mph (48km/h) – in around twenty minutes – a novice rider will be aiming to be close to 20mph (32km/h), or thirty minutes, so a manageable time frame.

Club evening events will also allow you to learn the ropes in terms of etiquette, pacing and the like in preparation for your first Open event.

As with road racing, you need to enter Open time trial events well in advance. The CTT website lists the events by region so you'll need to be a bit intuitive to find out which is your local region. Again, ask at the local shop or cycling club. Each course has a code too, so local information sources are invaluable. Riding up and down the A1 on a Sunday morning for your first Open event is probably not the best idea. It would be better to find a 10-mile time trial local to you on quieter roads. The website gives the event organizers' phone numbers, so you can phone for address details or check in a CTT handbook, which lists all the courses and events and gives organizers' details. Entry forms can be downloaded from the website or your local club will keep a stock. On-line entry is likely to become available in the near future.

There are many time trials across the UK that are even easier to enter and these are called club events. The principle behind these is that clubs run time trials, usually over the 10 or 25-mile (40km) distances, often in the evening. These are predominantly for the club's own members, but they will normally take riders from other clubs. These events are all 'entry on the line' and are normally very cheap. The only real difficulty will be finding the events. Your cycling club or local cycling shop will be the best place to find out where these races occur, as the venues can be a little obscure and tricky to find without local knowledge.

CHAPTER 6
Pre-Race Preparation and the Big Day

Now that you've identified the type of event you wish to enter, training becomes vital. The following will given you an idea of what to expect in your first training races.

WHAT TO EXPECT AT A CLUB EVENING TIME TRIAL

When you turn up at your first club evening 10-mile (16km) time trial it will help if you know what to expect; similarly for a handicap training race. Ideally, go along the week before your first training race simply to observe and get to know a few people. For the club evening time trials you will need to find out the course in advance. You can then ride the route a few times to familiarize yourself with the terrain and, importantly, the turns. At both types of event you will quickly see that there are riders of all shapes and sizes and a multitude of different bicycles.

At the time trial, there will be some riders on standard bicycles with drop handlebars and ordinary spoked wheels. Others will be riding very expensive looking time-trial-specific cycles with disc wheels and other carbon configurations. Some of the riders will be wearing normal cycling shorts and top along with an open-vented helmet. Others might be wearing one-piece suits and aero-shaped helmets. Some riders might not be wearing helmets at all as, at present, these are not compulsory although strongly recom-

mended. There are certain exceptions to this ruling – all under eighteens must wear a proper helmet and in certain regions local regulations stipulate proper helmet use.

CTT regulations stipulate that you must wear cycling-type shorts that come about halfway down your leg and your jersey must have at least short sleeves. Triathlon-type

RIGHT: *You don't need a fancy bike to ride your first time trial.*

OPPOSITE: *Michael Hutchinson – top UK time trial rider at all distances.*

Cycling shorts, a not-too-baggy jersey and a helmet are all the clothing you really need.

racing suits with vest tops, or swim trunks/football shorts and the like are not allowed. You should also be wearing either the club's official kit or a plain top. Although you would probably get away with wearing the pro-team replica kit of your cycling hero's team in a club or come-and-try-it type event, you certainly won't be able to in an Open event so you might as well start as you mean to go on and get used to race-pace work in your racing kit.

Bike-wise, as long as the bike is roadworthy, the type and style is pretty free. The best option for the novice is the standard road type of bike with the option of the clip-on time trial or tri-bars added.

The actual process of a club event involves getting there about thirty minutes or more before the event starts and completing the signing-in process – the registration. You will then be given a race number. This should be pinned to the back of your jersey near its base using safety pins. These are normally pro-

vided, but it is always worth having some spares available.

As a novice, you are likely to be set off early in the field so you won't need to worry about keeping the timekeeper or marshals waiting as you should be finished ahead of the later starters ... hopefully!

Make a mental or written note of your start time and follow the other rides down to the starting area. Ride to the start area in a nice easy gear – probably on your inner ring. As you approach the start area, put the bike into a gear you will be able to set off in. In practice, and depending on the terrain of the road ahead, this might well be on the bigger front chain ring and one of the bigger rear sprockets.

Make sure you are at or very near the start about five minutes before your due set-off time. Always check your watch against the time that others are setting off at. For example, if you are number fourteen, check your watch when number four starts, as you

Standard spoked wheels are easier to handle on windy days and the aero helmet reduces drag.

will be off exactly ten minutes later. If you miss the start time you will be penalized and the amount of time you were late by will be added to your race time.

Listen carefully for the timekeeper calling the riders before you as you stand in line. Remember, many of these time trials are held on the open road, so beware of road traffic and keep off the highway when not actually riding.

As the rider before you heads off down the road and into their race, take your bike up to the start line. Let the starter know your number and name; you can also point out that it is your first race. Normally, riders are held upright at the start, but you might prefer to set yourself off in your first race. However, remember in the Open event proper you might want to aim at using a held start, so in one of your training club events you'll need to practise this.

If being held, clip one foot in and stand astride the bike. At around thirty seconds to go – the timekeeper will keep you updated – the starter will ask you to get onto the saddle as they firmly hold your bike. Relax and don't fight the bike as you clip into the other pedal. Do clip both feet in, otherwise you are very likely to knee yourself in the chin when you set off. Trust the starter – very few have dropped a rider so you are unlikely to be the first, especially if you relax and don't fight the bike. Make sure one of your feet is at about the 2 o'clock position, ready for the off.

The timekeeper will announce fifteen seconds to go, then ten, then will count down five–four–three–two–one and GO. Sometimes the holder will rock you slightly back on five, three and one ready to give you a little extra help at the start – again don't panic, just relax. On GO you simply ride off down the road, often out of the saddle to get up to speed. Don't go mad – just increase your pedalling rate, sit down and increase leg speed a bit more before clicking into a faster gear and into your race.

It might be a good idea to have some practise starts, for example in a closed car park one evening. This will give you the confi-

The helper will hold you securely, so don't panic.

dence you need to relax whilst in the starter's hands. If you do decide to self-start, just remember not to go before the timekeeper says so!

Remember the aim of your training races are to practise pace strategy and get used to the physical experience of riding at race effort. On your first outing, keep the pace manageable. Work at the sort of rate you feel you can sustain, although it will be hard, you will be out of breath and your legs will hurt. Try to keep the gearing such that you can ride at around 80–90rpm. On hills, change to an easier gear so that you don't overdo the effort involved. On the downslope, remember you are still racing so avoid freewheeling if possible.

Other road users should be aware that a cycle event is taking place as warning signs will have been strategically placed on the course and course approaches. Nevertheless, you should exercise the same caution as you would when riding on the open road.

Although clubs usually have a marshal to indicate the turns, this isn't always the case so make sure that you are familiar with the route in advance.

Most events use a roundabout to turn, so take care. This should be the sort of manoeuvre you've done many times in training, but be aware that traffic might not expect you to be doing what is essentially a U-turn. Change into an easier gear as you approach the turn so that you can control the bike better and also can accelerate more easily once you are on the return leg.

As you approach the finish, remember to shout your number to the timekeeper as you pass. After passing the finish, you can pop the chain onto the inner, smaller chain ring and a nice easy gear ratio. Ride past the finish area, stopping when safe to do so, then make your way back to the club room or race headquarters. Remember you will feel tired and maybe a bit giddy, so don't rush – give yourself time and be safe. Often clubs have safety rules relating to no U-turns in the start or finish area, so be aware of these and follow the route taken by other riders.

When you get back to the club headquarters take off your number, stow your bike securely

ABOVE AND BELOW: Stay calm and focused as you set off down the road.

LEFT AND BELOW: Stay out of the saddle until you've got your speed up.

LEFT: If you prefer, you can start with one foot down.

Other road users should be aware that a cycle event is taking place.

Look out for the sign and hopefully a marshal to indicate the turn.

OPPOSITE: Take care as you approach the roundabout.

ABOVE: Remember to come off your tri-bars as you negotiate the roundabout.

and return your number to the officials. If you are lucky, you'll get a cup of tea and some biscuits or homemade cake (one of the joys of time trials) whilst you wait for the results.

Make a note of your time and the winner's time in your log book, plus any other points of note that might be a useful aide-memoire for future races. If you are planning to use time-trial-type bars, it makes sense to do the first training club event without them and then practise riding on them in other speed sessions. You might start off on the indoor trainer then progress to a traffic-free car park or similar. Finally, you might try them in a club event where, by now, you will be familiar with the course and the road surface. If unsure, it is preferable to stay with conventional bars and progress onto the time trial bars as your confidence increases.

WHAT TO EXPECT AT A CIRCUIT RACE TRAINING SESSION

As with the club time trial so with the road race training events; take yourself along one week to see what goes on and introduce

ABOVE: *Sharing the workload helps keep up a good pace.*

BELOW: *Hills are a favourite place for fitter riders to break away so be aware.*

ABOVE: Practise your group riding skills with one or two friends. BELOW: *Getting ready for the off.*

A chequerboard or flag usually indicates the finish – shout your number to the timekeeper nice and loud!

Take care when riding back to the headquarters.

yourself. Make notes on what sort of race exercises the group goes through and whether there are any exercises you can practice on your own in advance.

When you turn up for your first race training session make sure you bring your helmet, as this will be compulsory, and also that your clothing is appropriate – so no loose-fitting trousers or laces. A long sleeve top is probably a good idea and cycling gloves to protect against any spills.

Typical exercises that a race training session might involve include bunch riding skills – riding closer and closer together – and echelons – riding in a line across the track to take shelter from the wind. Expect there to be jargon such as 'through and off' or 'bit and bit' (*see* below).

The biggest difference between the solo riding effort of a time trial and bunch riding in a road race is the drafting – sitting in the slipstream of another ride. This is strictly forbidden in time trialling, but is essentially what road racing is all about.

Within your training you should have practised sitting in close behind the rider in front, perhaps on club rides or just out training with one or two friends. Practise at slower speeds in training and then increase the speed within your race training sessions. You will need to think about where the wind is coming from and adjust your position in relation to the other riders based on the wind direction. Obviously when you are riding on the open road safety issues and other traffic compromise this, so these race training sessions on closed circuits are ideal for honing your drafting technique.

If the wind is directly head on, the best shelter is directly behind the rider. If it's a cross wind, you should sit behind but to one side of the other rider – remembering that the forward motion of the front rider creates a slipstream effect in its own right. It is one thing practising drafting behind a single rider, but in a race everyone is going to be trying to sit in the same posi-

Watch out for that group behind – it's catching you.

tion, so you need to practise both in small groups and larger ones.

'Through and off' is an exercise in which the riders are in a long line and the front one peels off to the left or right, then eases down in speed, drifting to the back of the line to rejoin it. The new front rider stays on the front for just a short time before moving to the same side as the previous rider and slipping to the back of the line. Thus, the front rider is constantly changing, with the other rides taking shelter in the line. This means everyone does an equal amount of work on the front without overtiring.

When it is your turn at the front, just keep riding at the same speed as you were when in the line – don't accelerate – then look over your right shoulder and, if clear, pull over to the right (left shoulder if riders are pulling off to the left). Ease off on the pedals slightly so that your speed drops. Continue pedalling, albeit slightly easier than before, and look out for the line coming through on your left (if you pulled right).

Be ready for the last rider coming and then nip back into their slipstream. This is quite hard to judge and you'll need to dip into your energy reserves to make the effort, but once you are back into the slipstream you can relax a bit. Remember when riding on someone's wheel to stay close, but not too close! Focus on their seat post area rather than their rear wheel and, most importantly, do not overlap wheels.

'Bit and bit' is essentially the same technique, but the front rider tends to stay there for longer. Through and off can also be referred to as 'chain ganging' or 'two lines', so if you hear these being shouted they mean the same thing.

The race training session may include some handicap racing. As a novice, you could be in the first group off, so be ready. Make sure you are in an appropriate starting gear – similar to that shown in the time trial information above – but be mindful of the terrain. If it's an uphill start you might need to be in your inner chain ring.

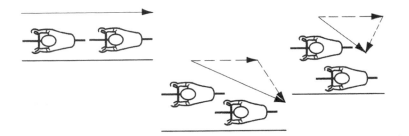

ABOVE: The best position to sit behind a rider for maximum shelter depends on the wind direction.

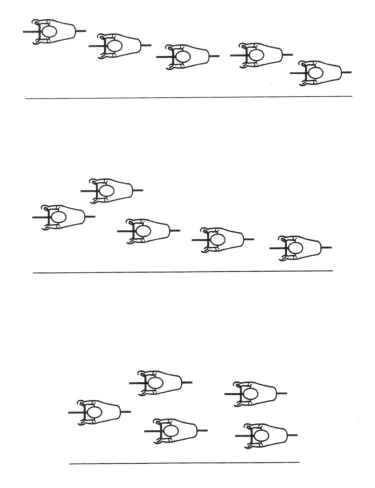

THREE ILLUSTRATIONS ABOVE: 'Bit and Bit' or 'Through and Off' are road race techniques worth learning.

OVERLEAF: The pace can be quite manic at the start of the race.

In road racing, you always start with one foot on the ground and so have to clip the other foot into the pedal at speed. This definitely needs practising. Experiment as to which starting leg you prefer and remember it! Make sure the starting foot is firmly clipped in and the pedal at the 2 o'clock position. Check there is no grit or mud on the other foot. As you set off, you might need to do a couple of pedal revolutions with the second foot resting on the pedal until you've got enough momentum to clip into the pedal properly.

The idea of the handicap race is that you get used to racing, but in smaller groups. Remember what you've practised during the training session and work together as a group to stay ahead of the chasers. Do your share of the work at the front of the group, but let others have a go too. If and when your group gets caught by the faster riders, be prepared. The speed will go up and again you will have to dip into your reserves until the pace settles down. Try to maintain a position near the front of the, now bigger, group, because if you drop to the back you will find the pace changes are exaggerated and the yo-yo effect makes life very difficult. As any seasoned road racer will tell you, it is easier to ride in the first half dozen or so riders, as the pace is smoother, than it is to be dangling near the back of the bunch.

Typically, these types of training races are very short, so listen for instructions. You may get the opportunity to practise sprinting for the line during the race training sessions and may alsol have played at sprinting on training rides with your friends. This means that when you get to the end of the race and the finish line is in sight, you can have a go. It is always worth sprinting for the line, even if you are in a group of four near the back … one day you may get the opportunity to sprint for a race placing and it helps to have practised this beforehand. Some riders prefer to sprint from a long way out – up to 1km (0.6 miles) (often marked with a flag), whilst others like to shoot out at high speed very close to the line. You will need to find out what sort of finish you prefer, but it helps to have a broad repertoire of race tricks.

Finally, use any debrief after the session to ask questions whilst you have the coaches there.

THE LAST FEW WEEKS OF TRAINING: PREPARING YOURSELF

So far, you've identified your first race event proper (circuit race or open time trial) and joined any necessary clubs or organizations. You've also identified some training events, such as handicap races or race training sessions at your chosen road race circuit venue or local club evening time trials. Hopefully, you've also given yourself plenty of time so that you can taper your training appropriately and ensure everything, including you and your bike, are ready on the day.

In the training section in Chapter 4 we looked at how training should be split into blocks, first building base fitness and cycling endurance before adding in some race-specific speed in the last few weeks prior to the event. The precise nature and timing of the speed element of the training will depend on how often you intend to race, but for the purposes of this first event we will stick with the seven–five–three block training model used in Chapter 4, giving us three weeks of final event-specific preparation. These last three weeks actually consist of two speed-oriented training weeks, plus one week where we focus on tapering for the race.

The two speed-oriented weeks will need to include some work at race pace, be that as a solo effort for time trialling, or within a group race training ride for road race practice. It is a good idea to include two or three speed-based sessions per week during this two-week block. One of these sessions might be a handicap race event or a club evening time trial over a similar distance to your main race event. Another session should involve shorter periods of harder and faster pace work – for example, riding for ten minutes hard (zone 4 effort) repeated three times, with a good recovery in-between for time trial practice, or six or seven different three-minute hard efforts up hills, out of corners and along straights as road race training.

If you haven't done so already, it might be a good idea to invest in a cycle computer that shows speed, distance and ideally cadence, as this will help with pacing your training and racing. At this stage, your training should be based on speed, cadence and perceived effort, so save purchasing a heart-rate monitor and other high-tech devices for later.

THE FINAL PREPARATION

Race entered, a couple of weeks of speed-specific training completed, some training race events ridden and race skills practised; now we enter the final week prior to the main event – your first Open time trial or road race.

We need to focus on three key elements to ensure that you arrive on the start line in the best possible mental and physical state:

- training and nutrition to prepare the rider
- checking over and preparing the bike
- checking over kit and what to take with you.

Preparing the Rider

Let's assume your event takes place at the weekend; if not, you'll need to juggle things around a bit. During the previous two weeks or so, your riding has been more focused on speed and should have included some training events. During this final week, maintain the speed focus until at least mid-week, possibly shortening the sessions but keeping them fast. From Thursday onwards, reduce both the duration and the intensity of the sessions but retain an element of leg speed. For example, Thursday's ride might be forty-five minutes on the inside ring and an easy gear, keeping the leg speed above 90rpm. Friday couldl be a proper rest day, with a short session on Saturday prior to Sunday's race. For a Saturday race, you should make Thursday your rest day and do a short pre-race session on Friday.

One good pre-race session would be what is called 'ten–ten–ten'. Ride nice and easy for ten minutes to warm up, then do ten minutes at one-minute high cadence (above 90rpm), one-minute easier cadence (around 75rpm); repeat this five times; then ten minutes' easy

riding to finish. The session should leave your legs tingling, but not tired.

In terms of nutrition, keep to your normal training diet. As you will be reducing the training load, you could cut back a bit on the total intake, but not too much as you need to make sure the energy stores are full before you start the race. Make sure you keep the hydration levels up, so drink plenty of water or your homemade hypotonic formula. Avoid alcohol and reduce your caffeine intake over the last four or five days, again to make sure the muscles are properly fuelled and hydrated without anything nasty in them.

Fuelling prior to an afternoon event is relatively straightforward, for example a simple but high-carbohydrate breakfast with some extra protein such as a smoothie or egg dish, followed by a light snack around three hours before the race. You can then keep topped up by using an energy drink alternated with plain water. It makes sense to have tried out your race-day meals in training, maybe by scheduling in a hard session one Saturday afternoon to mimic the race effort. If you get a stitch in the session this usually indicates that you ate too close to the session and/or the food was hard to digest. Switch to simpler, plainer low-fat foods and eat a bit earlier. You will know whether you've got the hydration right as the urine will be very pale – and with pre-race nerves expect to see plenty of it.

For a morning event, fuelling is a bit more difficult. Obviously, a high-carbohydrate but simple meal the night before makes sense, rather than a greasy fish and chip supper or a spicy curry. Pasta or rice and chicken in a plain sauce work well, with a milk-based dessert such as rice pudding or fruit and custard to follow. Plenty of water or hypotonic drink are necessary to ensure you are fully hydrated – you could take a bottle to bed for drinking if you wake in the night.

In the morning, you will need to rise early to ensure you are wide awake for the race and also to get in some pre-race food. Cereal, rice pudding or a white bread banana sandwich are all good fuels, but as with the Saturday race plan try out your pre-race regime in training. You might also use one of the special sports formulas designed for the pre-

Both you and your bike need to be in tip-top condition.

race period to ensure enough protein and carbohydrates have been ingested.

Also, make up a bottle of energy drink – with slightly less powder but the same amount of water to make it more dilute – to drink on the way to the event. You might also nibble on an energy bar or low-fat cereal bar on the way to the event, but make sure it is one you know won't give you stomach cramps by using a familiar brand. Some riders like to have a cup of coffee before setting off to an event to wake themselves up. This is fine so long as it is not taken to excess, as the caffeine can dehydrate the muscles, making you more prone to cramps.

Preparing the Bike

One golden rule of racing – whether you are a novice or a world champion – is never to try any-

thing new in an important event. This applies not just to food and drink, but also includes bike kit, clothing, strategies and the like.

Make sure your bike is in good working order. By all means get it serviced and replace worn tyres and any tubes that have previously been punctured and repaired, but make sure you ride it and check it under race load before the event. If you are using a different pair of wheels for the race then get them fitted and ride them under race load mid-week. One good tip is to pump the tyres up to race pressure – normally around 100psi for racing tyres – a few days before to check there are no slow punctures. You'll need to top the pressures up before the race again, but the tyres should have remained fairly hard. Note, though, that if your bike has tubular tyres or latex inner tubes it is normal for these to lose pressure faster than standard tyres, but again they should remain fairly hard overnight.

Give your bike a good clean and polish. Not only will it look better and ride more smoothly, but whilst cleaning it you can check over for nicks in the tyres, frayed cables and worn brake blocks. Check that the bolts on things like the seat pin and saddle clamp are tight, as well as the ones holding the handlebars and particularly any clip-on TT bars. Again, don't do this at the last minute in case you find something that needs professional servicing. Check your bike computer is working, especially if you've changed wheels, as the speed magnet might need to be fitted on. This is less important for a road race, as you need to be focusing on the race, but nevertheless you don't want magnets clipping sensors or cables hanging loose.

Check the spares kit in your under-saddle bag. Whilst you will need to carry some spares, you need not race with the same level of spares as you might carry on a winter training ride. For a time trial on the open road you need to be able to get back to race headquarters in the event of mechanical problems or a puncture; similarly, for a road race on the open road. For a circuit race, the distance back to the headquarters is not as far, so you might get away with leaving your spares kit in the changing room, but maybe better safe than sorry.

For a race you should carry:

• spare inner tube
• tyre levers
• lightweight mini multi-tool (optional)
• pump and/or carbon dioxide gas canister.

Realistically, this is a get-you-back-to-headquarters kit only – because if you do get a puncture that will be the end of your race for today. You also need to pack and check over your race kit bag at least the day before in case there is anything that you've mislaid.

Preparing the Kit

In this section, we will focus on ensuring that all the peripherals are in place for a successful race day. Check and recheck that you have covered everything, using the tick-off sheet at the end of this section as a guide. There are three key elements to this section:

• race kit – clothing, shoes, helmet and so on
• race bag kit – all the other things you need to take with you
• travelling kit – for to and from the event .

You should have already done some training in your race kit to ensure it is comfortable. Confirm in advance that it conforms to the regulations – short or long sleeves and mid-thigh length shorts and no trade team logos.

Check that your shoe plates (cleats) aren't worn or cracked and all the screws are tight. If in doubt, replace them a few days before the race, ensuring you fit the same type of cleat in the same place – draw around the old ones with a marker pen before removing them. Grease the new screws and double-check they are tight. Do a short ride to check the alignment is correct and then recheck for tightness. You don't want your plates coming loose during the event.

Pack your race clothes into your kit bag along with an undervest. It is always better to wear double layers, as not only will modern technical undervest materials aid temperature control, but the second layer will provide some protection in the event of a crash. Don't forget your socks and cycling shoes. Put the latter into a bag so that they don't mark the rest of your kit. Pack a spare jersey or additional vest in case it is cold, plus long tights and a long-sleeved top for your warm-up ride. If you tend to sweat a lot you should take a spare undervest, so that you can warm up in one and put a dry one on for the race itself. On top of these, pack your helmet. For all road races the rule of 'no helmet, no ride' applies. Helmet, shoes and licences are the pieces of kit most often forgotten, so don't be caught out!

You should also have in your kit bag a small washbag containing safety pins, embrocation – if you use it – Vaseline (helps to prevent shoes rubbing if this is a problem), cream for your shorts or undercarriage and, if appropriate, your asthma inhaler. Although inhaler-type asthma drugs are on the banned list of drugs in sport,

Race Day Checklist

Under-saddle Wedge Bag
Tyre levers	lightweight mini-tool
Pump and /or	CO2 gas canisters
Identification card	spare inner tube

Kit Bag
Helmet	cycling shoes
Shorts	socks
Undervest/s	cycling shorts
Race licence	personal identification
Race jersey	long-sleeved warm-up top
Long-legged tights	arm-warmers if available
Waterproof top	gilet (optional)
After-race tracksuit	after-race warm clothing
Energy drinks including recovery drink	gels and energy bars for afterwards
Fresh water	pen and notepad (for results)

Washbag
wet wipes/flannel	safety pins
Embrocation – optional	Vaseline
Chamoix cream – optional	asthma medication (if applicable)
Toilet tissues	wet wipes
Towel/s	soap/flannel

Others
Bike	Wheels, including spare pair if possible
Floor pump if available	additional tools and spare shoe plate if available
Race directions	start sheet

OPPOSITE: *Some riders prefer to warm up on their turbo trainer, especially before a time trial.*

Time trial bikes – built for speed in a straight line.

if you have been prescribed such preparations by your doctor for asthma then you qualify for what is known as a TUE – Therapeutic Use Exception. Your doctor will be able to give you a note to this effect if required.

At a race, there will be up to a hundred or so riders all wanting to use the bathroom and 'supplies' often run short, so carrying your own tissues is advised.

Pre-prepare the drinking bottles you need, including ones for the journey to and from the event. An old-fashioned milk bottle holder or a supermarket wine carrier are good for holding cycle bottles upright , otherwise they may leak if lying down with the bike in the back of the car. Pack some energy bars as well to snack on during the journey – remembering the golden rule of using only products you've tested during training.

If you use a floor-standing pump, take that with you as it will make pumping up the tyres so much easier. For a morning event, pump up the tyres before you leave home, but travelling in the afternoon in a hot car with tyres at race pressure is not to be recommended. Best to do the final pump-up as part of your pre-race routine.

For time trials and most road races you will have been sent a start sheet and possibly other information. Make sure you have read this thoroughly and don't forget to keep it somewhere accessible on your journey.

For time trials you will need to familiarize yourself with the course route. The race will normally be well signed and marshalled at the turns, but the onus is on the rider so check and double-check the route. Try to find out the distance and route from the headquarters to the start in advance. With on-line maps this task is very straightforward; otherwise use a good road atlas.

For circuit races, read through the course details to find out things like the length – whether time- or distance-based – and the terrain. Ideally, of course, you will have done a reconnaissance ride over the course as part of your pre-race training.

Finally, and very importantly; for time trialling in Scotland and road racing everywhere you will need to have your race licence with you, so keep it in a side pocket of your kit bag and check it's there before you leave home. It is also prudent to keep some form of identification in your under-saddle tool bag and in your kit bag in case of emergencies.

Unless the event is very local, it is better to travel in comfortable loose-fitting clothing, such as a track suit or similar. You can change back into these after the race, so pack a towel and some wash items. Village halls with limited wash facilities are often used as race headquarters, so a pack of wet wipes or a bottle of water and a flannel are a useful addition to the kit bag.

Check and recheck you've got everything, but then don't forget the bike and wheels!

ARRIVING AT THE RACE

Make sure you get there in plenty of time. One hour before the start is a good guide. The road race programme will give the time of your event. For time trials there will be a start time for the event – the time the first rider sets off at, plus your own start time. You should aim to be there about one hour before your own start time. If in doubt, leave earlier as the last thing you want is to arrive in a panic. Sometimes finding the race headquarters is a bit difficult, especially if located at a remote village hall. Check in advance that you know where it is – phone the organizer for directions if these aren't included with the race start sheet.

As with your training events you'll need to sign in and collect your number. Take your licence with you as this will be required for road races and Scottish time trials. Register as soon as you get there, as you can then find out about the route to the start, any changes or special conditions, such as the no U-turns rule, and find out about the toilet and changing facilities.

OPPOSITE, TOP: At road races riders usually warm up on the circuit itself.
OPPOSITE, BOTTOM: In a time trial, keep your head up and focus on smooth pedalling.

Get yourself into your race kit with your number pinned onto your jersey and then put on an additional long-sleeved top and long training tights if it is cool. Set the bike up and pump up the tyres to race pressure. Check that the wheels are in the frame straight and not rubbing on the frame or brakes. Pop on your shoes and helmet and go for your warm-up ride. By now, you should have a routine that you've developed from studying other riders and have practised within your training sessions. A good routine is one based on the session you've used as your pre-race day leg looser: ten–ten–ten. You could amend this to be ten minutes of easy riding to get the legs moving after the journey, then around five to eight minutes of building to near race effort, followed by another five to eight minutes of easy riding. Around fifteen–twenty minutes of warm-up for a 10-mile time trial should be enough. Don't be tempted to do any more, or you'll be tired before you start the race.

For a circuit-based road race the warm-up usually involves riding around the course. Use your first ten minutes of easy riding to observe the course, mentally noting the terrain, the race line and any obstacles. Note especially the start so that you can choose your starting gear appropriately. Use the five–eight minutes of race pace riding to do a couple of laps faster to get a feel for the track, then cool down.

Before, during and after the warm-up, sip your energy drink. You would normally expect to have drunk around 500ml of energy drink (at either normal strength or slightly more diluted if it's hot) in the last hour before the race. Do sip it though – drinking the full 500ml just before you set off for the start is not a good idea.

Keep a close eye on the time, ensuring your watch is reading the same time as the official timekeeper's one.

After the warm up, take off your warm-up top and bottoms and change your undervest if desired. After a last minute trip to the bathroom make your way to the start, aiming to get there with around five minutes to go.

Sometimes, for road races, there will be a rider briefing, so listen out for this and take heed of the instructions and warnings. Alternatively, it might take the form of a written notice, so again look out for these and take note.

THE RACE ITSELF

As far as the race start itself goes, mentally rehearse the process – you've practised in training enough times. Make sure you clip your first foot in firmly and remember to have the lead foot at the 2 o'clock position before starting. At a time trial, if you still don't feel confident with the held start then ask to have a foot-down start – you won't be the only one. In a road race, try to start fairly near the middle of the group and in the middle of the track. This will give you more space to manoeuvre once you set off.

In a time trial, the pacing is down to you, so keep things under control. Think about headwind versus tailwind and adjust your target speed accordingly. The biggest mistake riders make is to start too quickly. Lactic acid builds up in the muscles and you pay the price in the long run. Use your gears to keep the cadence in the 80–95rpm range – maybe a little but not much lower on the hills.

Keep your head up and watch where you are going – safety takes precedence over speed. There will be other traffic on the road and they may not expect you to be going as fast as you are, so keep your wits about you. Take care, especially at the turn, and after the finish ensure you find somewhere safe to stop. You must shout your number to the timekeeper at the end, so it makes sense to note where the finish is in relation to the start.

For road races, the pace will probably not be under your control. The start is often the most manic part of the race, so really dig deep and hang in there. After a while, it will settle down and you can catch your breath. Sometimes, a group goes off up the road as a breakaway group and then the remaining riders in the main bunch settle down in pace. Wherever possible, aim to keep in the front half of the group and away from the gutters.

ABOVE: In a fast-moving bunch the riders get strung out in a line.
BELOW: Gather round the results board and meet the other riders.

Personal Race Notes						
Date	Event	Course	Personal Time or Position	Winner's name	Winner's time	Notes
10/8	Wobbly wheelers 10 TT	Z10-1	29–29 (15th out of 16)	Fred Fast – CC Cycling	21–12	Windy day but pleased
21/07	CC Cycling Criterium	Hillingdon circuit	15th (out of 20)	Joan Bloggs – CC Cycling		Fast race – got dropped

If you end up getting dropped by the main bunch, don't despair. Look around for other riders with whom you can regroup and then use your through-and-off practice experience to get riding strongly again. You might catch up with the bunch, or at least pick up some more stragglers along the way.

The procedure if you get lapped will depend on the race regulations and this should have been made clear in the rider briefing. Often you can join back into the bunch (if you are physically able to) and continue racing, which is great for additional experience and training. You may have to drop out, say, three laps before the finish. At some courses, however, lapped riders are eliminated. It therefore pays to do your homework.

AFTERWARDS

After the race, make your way back to the changing rooms or headquarters. Hand back your number and, if appropriate, collect your race licence.

Enjoy the post-race atmosphere – it is a good time to learn about tactics and performances and also to pick up some of the jargon, as well as meet new friends. Use your recovery drink and energy bars to put back in the energy you've expended and help your recovery post-race. By all means take advantage of any post-event catering, but having your own tried-and-tested post-race drink and bars is a safe standby.

At road races there is often a prize presentation and social gathering for which you should stay. You rarely get an official results sheet, but the top placings can be found later in the results section of the British Cycling website. At time trials the results are posted on a results board during the course of the event. Sometimes there is a prize presentation, but more often prizes are sent out to the winners along with the results sheet, which is sometimes also posted on the CTT website.

For all events keep a note of the date, course, winner and your time and/or position. Apart from needing this information for entering future events, it will also form an interesting and informative record of your progress. It also makes sense to add in some notes relating to the experience so that you can learn as you go along.

Include in the notes some things that went well and what you need to work on for next time. Remember that many of your fellow riders may have been competing for years and may all know each other. It may therefore take time for you to be fully integrated into the social post-race chat and to understand all the jargon, but you've made the first step so enjoy the experience. Who knows, you might even soon be a prize winner. Many time trial events have a second prize category based on handicap. Depending on your previous performances, a time allowance is taken off your race time, with slower riders getting a bigger allowance than faster ones. Essentially, this system rewards the rider who has made the biggest improvement – one day this could be you.

CHAPTER 7
What Next?

By following the guidelines in this book, you are now fitter and a lot faster. You have developed your bike riding skills and ridden your first race, either a time trial or road race. Welcome to the world of the competitive cyclist.

Hopefully your experience of competing was a positive one. If not, you must ask yourself why. Did you pick the right type of event? Did you prepare as well as you could? Did you have the right equipment for the race on the day? All of your experiences can be learnt from, helping you to develop as a rider, achieve your goals and become a competent racer who will enjoy the racing experience.

It is those goals that we will reflect on here. Racing a bike is a wonderful way to stay fit and healthy, but it can be a frustrating hobby without some direction. You will be aware of the category system and for road racing this can be a good way to incentivize yourself for a longer period. There can be advantages to targeting specific events as the system is open all year and you may have peaks and troughs in this period that affect the way you race. You may also experience a 'bad day', which is not unusual if you are juggling your sport with family and work commitments. With time trialling, there are a number of local series or leagues and these can provide regular competition in a friendly environment where everyone can succeed in their own way. Using a course on a regular basis can also provide you with an ongoing challenge to improve your personal best; this can often be a lifelong battle.

Progressing through the categories can prove a very tangible way of measuring your improvements. You will have started off as a fourth-category rider and unless you were very successful in your first race (you would need to have won it!), it will be necessary to find some more races to enable you to score some more points and progress to the next category. There have been some riders in the UK who have progressed from the fourth category through to elite rider in one season, but this is very rare as it would require wins in the first few races to progress through the categories so quickly. More realistic aims are to score a set number of points, or to achieve a certain category within a given space of time. Either of these will provide a large goal for a long period of time, which can carry you through the natural peaks and troughs in your form as you train race and continue with a life outside of cycling. This longer-term goal can also accommodate a number of smaller goals along the way, for example a specific result such as a top-ten finish, or it may encompass some other competition as well, which we will discuss later. Not everyone is going to be able to become a second, first or elite category rider. It may be that your natural talent and the amount of time you have available for training will allow you to become a good second or third category rider, but you don't manage to progress to the next category, or, if you do, struggle to stay in it for successive seasons. If this proves to be the case, it will be best to rethink your approach and bring your goals in line with your abilities and available time. This may be as simple as targeting a certain number of points scored in a year, or you may start to look beyond the road race licence points as your method of incentive.

Many regions have different types of road race league. The formats are very varied and

The time trial rider gets underway.

often include specific races, such as handicap races in which riders of different ages or categories set off at different times. This kind of racing allows riders of different abilities to compete against each other. Other types of league allow riders of the same category to race on a regular basis. At the end of the league season, a table will be presented – a valuable goal would be to target a position in the overall table. With many leagues giving points to riders for finishing, as well as for achieving placing, this provides an incentive to keep racing in the league.

There is an increasing amount of racing taking place for the more mature athlete, with age-group racing and time trials for riders over forty common in the UK, or there may be specific prizes for older riders. These races often operate as handicap races, with younger age groups setting off last. Sometimes the races are all-category mass starts, although this makes it difficult for race orga-

nizers at the finish line as they have to establish the placings in every age group. If racing in this type of event, it is important to keep going right up to the line. Race placings can be targeted either overall or within a personal age group, thus providing a number of ways in which to set targets. There are many mature athletes who seem to get faster as they get older, so age should not be a barrier to improving standards.

Your aspirations may be to head for foreign shores and every year there are many cyclists who go abroad to train and race, with Majorca and Lanzarote proving popular for training, whilst Belgium and France are the top venues for amateur racing abroad. Local cycling clubs can usually provide information. Again, there is a lot of racing for riders of all ages, with Belgium being especially veteran-friendly.

With time trials there is a very simple way of challenging yourself and that is to record

Getting to the start line on time is important.

a faster time for a set distance. This is effective for many people, although it can be frustrating as fast times are often dependent on the weather and sometimes the traffic conditions. It is useful, therefore, also to consider some different ways of challenging yourself. Many local cycling clubs run their own race series. Similar to the road race series, it is about consistent performance and you will obtain an overall position at the end of the year.

There is a national competition for time trials called the British Best All Rounder (or BAR). This is based on some of the longer-distance triathlons and the result is taken from the average speed across the events. Entrants can choose which qualifying events to do and can therefore adapt the competition around their personal schedules. This is a long-standing competition and very prestigious for the winner.

There is also a circuit time trial series based on what is now referred to as a sporting course. This is a move away from the traditional out-and-back courses, often nicknamed drag strips. A circuit time trial will provide a better comparison to what is available on the continent and seen on television in the big tours. The weather and traffic will play a smaller part in these events. Time trialling of this type is increasing in popularity, both within the national series and with clubs organizing smaller events. Targeting a realistic position within time trials is a good way of racing. For example, you could target being in the top twenty in every Open time trial that you enter in a season. Succeeding in your personal goal would be a great achievement and a testament to your consistent training and performance.

Another approach, for a cyclist who has specialized in one of the particular areas, is to swap disciplines for a period of time. For example, a road racer will find an additional challenge in time trials, whilst the time trial rider will need to develop some new skills to be an effective road-racer.

There are a number of other types of cycle sport available that will certainly help with your road race or time trial cycling. Track cycling has become increasingly popular, especially in the UK, where Olympic and World Championship success has created a degree of interest. There is the obvious issue of finding a velodrome, either an outdoor one, or, more rarely, indoor, but if you are fortunate enough to live near such a facility you would be depriving yourself of a wonderful experience if you were not to take up the opportunity to have a go. Track racing requires only a simple bike, but many velodromes have bikes for hire and it is very easy to get on the track. You will probably need a little bit of tuition, but after this you are often free to race. Racing takes place at lots of different levels, with most tracks having a league that runs throughout the season, sometimes into the winter if the track is indoors. Popular leagues categorize riders according to age and ability, and there is often racing for children, thus allowing it to become a genuine family affair.

Track racing is very varied, from longer endurance races, often in mass groups, through to events such as the pursuit and the sprint events. This means that regardless of your particular ability, you should be able to find an event to suit you.

Off-road cycling covers two broad groups: Cyclo-Cross and mountain bike racing. Cyclo-Cross has seen an increase in partici-

pation over the last few years. This is partly due to young riders being directed towards fun, safe racing that also helps to develop bike handling and racing skills. These young people have often brought along parents who also wanted a go. Road riders are also finding Cyclo-Cross attractive as it means they can race all year, thereby satisfying their competitive urges throughout the calendar. Cyclo-Cross racing is normally organized into leagues, with both local and national leagues and national championships available for riders of all ages. The races are generally quite short and newcomers are always made to feel welcome.

Mountain biking has a number of different facets, broadly categorized into cross-country and downhill racing. Cross-country/endure racing is closest to the physical demands of road racing and time trialling, and is a great way to develop skills. As the name suggests, it is based on off-road cross-country courses and the terrain will generally be much more technical than in a Cyclo-Cross race. Racing takes place broadly in age categories, although the middle senior category can be a little wide. Distances vary, from the shorter standard race through to endure races of 25–100km. There are also some longer twelve and twenty-four-hour races that can be tackled solo, in a pair, or as a team of four or more riders. The road rider will often find that off-road cycling provides a great all-over body workout, which is a really positive aspect for all-round fitness.

Regardless of the type of racing you are interested in, club membership will prove useful and by tracking down a local cycling club you will access a wealth of information about where to race and when, as well as finding lots of new training partners and opportunities.

Finally, whatever path you decide to follow as your cycling develops, above all enjoy your cycling and enjoy racing.

How to Find Cycle Racing Events in the UK

Finding road races and time trials is not difficult and there a number of sources that will help you. In the old-fashioned style, there is a weekly magazine called *Cycling Weekly*. This magazine has been around for many years and normally hits the news stands on Thursday mornings. Towards the back of the magazine you will find a list of road races and time trials organized by date. The race organizer's details will be published, so that you can contact them to find out if you are eligible to race. As with many magazines, there is also a website version:
www.cyclingweekly.co.uk

British Cycling is the governing body for cycle sport in the UK. It has a large website which contains a great deal of information. Within this site, you can search for events by geographical location, type of event, date and category of event. This is a fantastic tool, as it enables the rider to search either for specific events or within general categories. This site is very useful, but lists only a few time trials as they are listed elsewhere.

British Cycling also publishes an annual handbook which contains most of the data available on the website and also sends out a magazine during the year with updates to the published calendar. Both the handbook and the magazine are membership benefits for those taking out the higher membership package from the organization. The competition rules are also included on the website: www.britishcycling.org.uk

Time trials are governed by an organization called Cycling Time Trials. This organization has been around for many years and is a little old-fashioned in the way it operates. It publishes a handbook every year and also has a website that contains most of the information in the handbook. The details of the annual handbook, normally available in January, can also be found on the website. The competition rules are also included on the website:
www.ctt.org.uk

The League International (TLI) organizes some road racing in the UK. Its coverage is not universal, but it does have a policy of making events easy to enter and take part in. You can join the TLI as a member and will receive some postal updates. The website also contains details of membership and the races taking place through the season. The competition rules are included on the website:
www.theleagueinternational.com

The League of Veteran Racing Cyclists is a membership organization that arranges road racing for cyclists over the age of forty. The website contains details of events and membership packages and, as with other websites, it contains the rules of competition events:
www.lvrc.org

Off-road events can be found on the British Cycling website, with all Cyclo-Cross events listed and some mountain bike events. Other mountain bike events can be found on the following two websites:
www.britishtrails.co.uk
www.singletrackworld.com

Other interesting websites for the aspiring
cycle racer which are worth a look are:
www.veloriders.co.uk
www.cyclingnews.com
www.ctc.org.uk
www.cycling.tv
www.sustrans.org.uk
www.bikeradar.com
www.usacycling.org
www.cyclingnz.com
www.cyclingforum.com

Glossary

Adaptation
The process of improving physical fitness by applying overload and resting.

Aero helmet
Protective headwear designed to reduce aerodynamic drag.

BMX
A mass-start off-road race based on a specific racing course designed for BMX racing. Very fast and very short races.

Bottom bracket
The chain set is attached to the crank via this part of the frame, which is at the very bottom of the frame and contains the bearings that allow the cranks to turn.

Cadence
The speed of pedalling measured in revolutions per minute.

Cassette
The name for the cogs at the rear of the bike on the rear wheel.

Chain ring
The name for the cogs that sit on the outside of the chain set.

Chain set
The large set of cogs at the centre of the bike to which the pedals are attached on one side.

Chamois
The inserted padded material inside the cycling shorts. No longer a proper chamois, but a synthetic replacement that does the same job.

Circuit race
A road race that takes place on a closed circuit over a number of laps.

Cleat
The attachment on the bottom of a specific cycling shoe which holds the shoe onto the pedal.

Club event
A time trial event that is organized by a club; normally open to other riders but not required to be. Often takes place in the evenings.

Commissaire
The cycling term for a race referee or official.

Criterium
The name for a circuit race used in France and around the world. Normally these races take place in urban areas using quite short circuits.

Cyclo-Cross
An off-road mass-start race normally over a number of laps of a course, with the winner being the first rider over the line.

Derailleur
The name for the mechanism that is used for moving the chain between the gears.

Down tube
The part of the frame that drops down from the front of the frame to the bottom bracket.

Frame
The main component at the heart of a bike.

Normally made up of two triangles, the larger one comprising the top, seat and down tube, and the rear triangle including the seat stays and chain stays.

Front forks
The items that fit into the frame and hold the front wheel in place.

Handlebars
The part of the bike that the rider holds onto with the hands.

Headset
At the front of the frame, the part to which the handlebars and stem attaches and pass though to allow steering of the bike.

Heart rate
Measured in beats per minute and an indicator of how hard a cyclist is working.

Helmet
Protective headwear.

Interval training
A term used to describe training at differing intensities. This is normally done by working very hard for a period of time then resting, sometimes for a set amount of time, and then repeating the process for a number of 'intervals'.

Lactic acid
The substance that is produced in the muscles when working very hard and which produces a 'burning' feeling.

Lactate threshold
The level of intensity that you can work at where your body is producing lactic acid but is also able to process the lactic acid so the build up is not an issue.

Mountain bike
A generic term for an off-road bike. Racing is categorized broadly into cross-country and downhill, with variations of this theme including 4X, marathon, endure and many others.

Neutralized section
A section of the race generally at the beginning where there is no racing taking part but the group is still moving.

Neutralized service
A vehicle that will provide a rider with mechanical assistance during a road race.

Open event
An event that must be entered in advance. Generally a term used in time trialling.

Overtraining
By training too much or resting too little, the body is not able to recover fully and the process of overtraining is started.

Personal best
A term commonly used in time trials to indicate the best time a rider has ever done, or, specifically speaking, the best time a rider has done in recent years.

Race licence
The document which allows participation in cycle road races; provided in the UK by British Cycling.

Ratio
The term used to describe a gear. This can be expressed as the number of inches or centimetres travelled for every pedal revolution, or can be expressed as the number of teeth on the chain ring/sprocket. For example, fifty-two teeth on the chain ring and twelve on cassette sprocket would be expressed as 52×12.

Rear drop-out
The part of the frame to which the rear wheel is directly attached.

Rear stays
Part of the stay that comes down from behind the saddle to the back wheel.

Road bike
The description given to a bike used for racing on the road. To the layman, described as a bike with curly handlebars.

Road race
A mass-start race over laps of a course or between two set points; the winner is the first across the line.

Rolling start
A practice used in time trials where the group will roll along at a steady pace before the race starts.

Saddle
The seat the rider uses when on the bike.

Seat post
The part of the frame that attaches the saddle via the seat pin to the frame.

Seat pin
The connecting component between the saddle and the frame.

Spokes
The small rod-like components that attach the wheels hub to the wheels rim where the tyre sits.

Sporting course
In time trials, a course that is not straight out and back and probably contains some climbs.

Stage race
A race that is run over a number of different stages, or races in their own right. Can include a time trai, but will also include road race stages as well. The Tour de France is a stage race.

Start sheet
A pre-printed sheet that gives the names and clubs of riders who have entered the event in advance. In time trials the start sheet will also give a start time.

Stem
The connecting component between the handlebars and the headset part of the frame.

Timekeeper
The term used for a person who officially notes the times at time trial events.

Time trial
A ride over a set distance, either solo or with a set number of riders (two, three or four), with the time deciding the winner.

Top tube
The part of the frame that runs horizontally along the top nearest to the rider.

Index